John William and Sophie Poe in 1884. Courtesy of the Western History Collections, University of Oklahoma Library.

Buckboard Days ⌣

by Sophie A. Poe

Edited by Eugene Cunningham
Introduction by Sandra L. Myres

University of New Mexico Press
Albuquerque

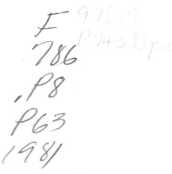

Library of Congress Cataloging in Publication Data

Poe, Sophie A. (Sophie Alberding), 1862–
    Buckboard days.

    Reprint. Originally published: Caldwell, Idaho: Caxton Printers, 1936.
    Includes index.
    1. Poe, John William, 1850–1923. 2. Poe, Sophie A. (Sophie Alberding), 1862–   . 3. Frontier and pioneer life—New Mexico. 4. New Mexico—History—1848–   . 5. Pioneers—New Mexico—Biography. 6. New Mexico—Biography. I. Cunningham, Eugene, 1896–1957. II. Title.
    F786.P8P63 1981   978.9'04'0922   [B]   80-54565

ISBN 0-8263-0572-5   AACR2
ISBN 0-8263-0573-3 (pbk.)

Manufactured in the United States of America. Library of Congress Catalog Card Number 80-54565 (clothbound) 0-8263-0572-5. International Standard Book Number 0-8263-0573-3.

This volume contains the complete text of the first edition, published in 1936 by the Caxton Printers, Ltd.

To that dauntless band of pioneers of the old Southwest, those who knew and loved my husband, this volume is most affectionately and appropriately dedicated.—SOPHIE A. POE.

Contents

List of Illustrations

☆

Introduction

IN HIS INTRODUCTION to the first edition of Sophie Poe's *Buckboard Days*, well-known Western
writer Eugene Cunningham emphasized the importance of the volume to a better understanding of the
Lincoln County "Wars" and the role of John William
Poe in the taming of the New Mexico frontier. For
Cunningham, and probably for most readers in the
1930s and 1940s, the principal appeal of the volume
was the story of John William Poe, buffalo hunter,
detective, United States Marshal, and sheriff, as he
tracked Billy the Kid, chased desperados, and brought
dangerous criminals to justice. But as Cunningham
noted, *Buckboard Days* is much more than an account of a wild and woolly chapter in frontier history, and it is more than a biography of a famous
lawman and his fight to bring law and order to a raw
frontier. It is also the story of a remarkable and
courageous woman, and it is this aspect of the book
which may have the greatest interest for today's
readers.

Sophie Poe was born in Petaluma, California, in
1862, the third of five children of Frederick Henry
and Rosanna Felker Alberding. Her earliest years
were evidently happy, although the family's life was
often unsettled. Alberding, a civil engineer, horse
breeder, and speculator, moved from job to job, from

venture to venture, always looking for the elusive pot of gold at the end of the next rainbow. When Sophie was ten, her father died. Her mother sold the Nicaragua plantation which was to have made their fortune and returned to California where the family owned and operated a chicken ranch. But within the year, Mrs. Alberding died of tuberculosis, and the children went to Illinois to live with a maternal aunt. The two boys soon drifted away to seek employment and adventure. The oldest, Fred, went to Roswell, New Mexico, to work on a ranch owned by a close family friend, Captain Joseph C. Lea. Sophie's oldest sister, Mary, married and established her own home, and Sophie and nine-year-old Edith went to live with her. Although she had a home, there was little for Sophie to look forward to. There were few prospects in rural Illinois for an orphaned girl with little formal education or training, and her future must have seemed bleak.

Then brother Fred wrote urging Sophie to join him in New Mexico. Ostensibly the purpose of the trip was simply a visit with a long absent brother. However, according to a family member, the real reason for the invitation was to "find Sophie a husband." So, with some trepidation, Sophie boarded a train for New Mexico, "a remote and fearsome place," described to her as "filled with savage Indians, wild horses, and bad men who took delight in killing each other."

To nineteen-year-old Sophie Alberding, New Mexico seemed to be the "jumping off place." The territory had a population of a little over 100,000, most of it Mexican-American. Although the completion of the Santa Fe railroad in 1879 had brought a new commercial vigor to the northeastern and central parts of the territory and provided a direct link to the rest of the nation, southeastern New Mexico was still a remote frontier. Lincoln County embraced 27,000 square miles of land, much of it still in the public domain. Free land and mining booms in the White Oaks and Nogal districts attracted not only ranchers and miners but a certain lawless element including gamblers, horse thieves, cattle rustlers, and gunmen. The scattered settlements at Roswell, White Oaks, and the county seat, Lincoln, were little more than small ranching and mining centers where people could get their mail, buy supplies, and enjoy a pleasant hour or two of sociability and companionship before returning to isolated farms and ranches. Schools, churches, and other amenities were still in the future.

Yet despite the remoteness of the area and her earlier fears, Sophie quickly came to love the country and its people. She admired and respected the Leas and other ranch families. As she became accustomed to their ways, she also made friends with cowboys and ranch hands. The single men of the area welcomed the attractive young woman, and she soon had many ardent admirers. She enjoyed horseback and buggy rides and the occasional dances and parties that helped to enliven life on that far-flung frontier. But although Sophie had a number of beaux, none "suited" her as a husband. Finally, Captain Lea took a hand. He decided that Sophie should marry, and he decided on a likely candidate. Needless to say, the independent and somewhat headstrong Sophie had other ideas—until she met the intended husband. Once she saw John William Poe, she wrote, "I realized then and there that 'the conqueror of the citadel' had come."

Within a few months of their first meeting, Sophie and John William were married, and set off for their new home in Lincoln. The story of the Poes' somewhat unorthodox courtship and marriage has become an oft-repeated tale in the history and folklore of Lincoln County. Poe was thirty-three, he had lived on the frontier most of his adult life, and he was used to doing things his own way. Sophie was twenty-one, gently reared despite her somewhat nomadic existence, and still unaccustomed to frontier ways. Yet despite the disparity in their ages and backgrounds, their marriage was a happy one.

During the first years of their marriage, the Poes lived on John William's ranch, the VV, twenty-five miles from Lincoln. Although Poe was often gone for long periods of time, Sophie enjoyed ranch life and learned to cope with hired hands, "wandering aborigines," and the lack of female companionship. Still, it was a lonely and sometimes frightening life. Sophie worried and waited for her husband to return, never knowing whether he might come home seriously wounded, or even dead, from an encounter with some fugitive from justice. In 1886, at Sophie's urging, John left law enforcement and thereafter devoted his considerable talents and energies to stock raising, agriculture, and banking. In all of these endeavors, Sophie was an enthusiastic, although silent, partner, admiring her husband's business acumen and supporting whatever decisions he made. Childless after the birth of a son who lived only a few days, John and Sophie found fulfillment in each other. They enjoyed traveling and made a number of trips abroad. They visited South America, made a tour of Europe, and in 1913 took a leisurely trip around the world.

When Poe died in 1925, Sophie was not only lonely but in reduced circumstances owing to financial reverses in Poe's banking investments. The traits of courage and adaptability that had helped her adjust to the new life she found in New Mexico in 1881 now stood Sophie in good stead, and she embarked on a new career. In 1916, she had published a little volume of travel reminiscences entitled *Ten Months on the Wing*. Although the book hardly met with great acclaim, or substantial sales, it helped preserve the memory of a happy time in her life. Now, faced with diminished financial and emotional resources, Sophie began to recall and recapture other parts of her life with John William. In 1933, she published *Nomading South of the Equator*, an account of her South American travels. In 1936, *Buckboard Days* appeared, written with the help of Eugene Cunningham. And in 1942, when Sophie was eighty years old, *Out of a Duffle Bag* completed her list of travel accounts.

Sophie Poe was an honest writer. Her style was simple, straightforward, and without the literary pretensions that often mar pioneer reminiscences. Because she had little formal education and no literary training, it is possible that the more technical passages (such as the method of tanning buffalo hides) and the spritely dialogue that enlivens some of the chapters may have been supplied by Cunningham. But Poe had a sense of place and history and a deep devotion to preserving the memory of the area and its people. She encouraged Lillie Klasner to prepare *My Girlhood Among the Outlaws* for publication, and she probably assisted other local writers.

When Sophie wrote *Buckboard Days*, her chief purpose was to tell the story of her husband and his role in many exciting and well-known events of New Mexico history. She wanted, she wrote, to "create a memoir" to "establish his achievements." And the chapters on John William's early life as a buffalo hunter and lawman and the sections on the Lincoln County War and the death of Billy the Kid are not without interest. But they are not the best chapters in the book. It is when Poe discusses the things she knows—the New Mexico landscape, the customs of her Mexican neighbors, the fears and triumphs of a young bride on an isolated frontier ranch—that she is at her best as historian and recorder. The most important parts of Poe's narrative are not the ofttold tales of gunfights and range wars but the simple phrases of a woman writing about the land and the people she knew and loved.

Buckboard Days is a good biography of a famous New Mexico pioneer, but it more than a memorial to a man. This is as much Sophie's story as it is John William's. It is a delightful, and often inspiring, account of a young woman's courage and perseverance, and it deserves to take its place among the other books by pioneer women that are at last becoming recognized as an important part of the literature and history of the American West.

Sandra L. Myres
The University of Texas at Arlington

Editor's Foreword

THIRTY YEARS AGO, it must be, that I first heard of John William Poe. His name was one of three mentioned by that old-timer who related vivid myth and even more lurid fact about the Lincoln County War. I came to know Sheriff Pat Garrett and Deputy John Poe and Desperado Billy the Kid long before I had seen the great pines along those lovely little rivers, the Bonito and Ruidoso, or walked down Lincoln's drowsy street.

As I began to accumulate information about New Mexico, more and more often I encountered the tall figure of John William Poe. For in the varied roles he knew he became a personage in his adopted state.

A quiet, forceful man, always unassuming, always dodging the spotlight of personal publicity, he was the finest type of frontiersman, looking to and building for the future while closely linked with the dangerous past.

For all these reasons, this simply told story of John Poe's life has held much interest for me. And for another reason it should hold interest for students of American life: it offers not only the history of a man who lived an incredibly full and active and valuable life, but also it mirrors in its every line the reaction to a frontier environment of a sensitive and cultured and observant woman who lived that same life.

For Mrs. Poe is a frontierswoman as her husband was a frontiersman. Her own full history would alone make an adequate and fascinating volume. Much of what she relates here she had both by hearsay from her husband and his associates and by personal observation. Her account of the Lincoln County troubles (often dignified nowadays by the term "War") and their aftermath, just for instance, represents a description and analysis built of the views and beliefs and experiences of many persons. It is perhaps the most rounded account yet to appear in print of this controversial and complicated subject, because of this peculiarity.

It has been a pleasure to edit Sophie Poe's chronicle. I, like many others who have spent years in digging out the facts of Western history, own the profoundest respect for John William Poe. Any account of his life seemed to me a belated and welcome tribute to a man deserving much of to-day's Southwesterners. And this account in particular, because of innate sincerity of approach and unquestionable authenticity of content, held me in its original form from beginning to end.

It was my effort throughout the work of editing to let Mrs. Poe tell her own story and by the combination of our labors to produce a book worthy of permanent place upon the shelf of Western sources, even of *Americana* in general.

EUGENE CUNNINGHAM.

Preface

IN THE PREPARATION of this volume I have tried to bring him whom, under the name of "John William," it chiefly concerns, as vividly as possible before my readers. Too, I have endeavored to show the characteristics of life in the remote southwestern corner of New Mexico during that period of time which may appropriately be termed "the buckboard days."

I am sure that in my chronicle are persons and events and places which enter into the history of the early Southwest in a large and significant way. If each of the experiences and activities of John William Poe could be recorded; if all his many roles in the development of his section could be adequately presented to show him "in full and true dimensions" as frontiersman, buffalo hunter, marshal, sheriff, detective, stockman, banker, capitalist, man-of-affairs, this volume would be much larger.

Even though such complete treatment is not possible, as his widow I have tried in this book to create a memoir which may establish his achievements "against the wreckful siege of battering days."

For their assistance in the preparation of my original manuscript, I offer my thanks to E. A.

Brininstool of Los Angeles and Major Maurice G.
Fulton of Roswell. Their advice was invaluable.
Ashley Pond Rollins constantly encouraged me to
persist in the work of collecting and preparing
data for the chronicle. E. A. Cahoon supplied his-
torical memoranda regarding the First National
Bank of Roswell. My thanks are also due to Noah
H. Rose of San Antonio and others who supplied
the photographs—some of which have never before appeared in a book—needed to make the
narrative more vivid.

SOPHIE A. POE.

Buckboard
Days ⌣

The Young Kentuckian Goes West

JOHN WILLIAM POE always said that Scott's *Waverly Novels* were chiefly responsible for his early wanderings and for those exciting experiences which were his lot on the Southwestern frontier.

"Twenty years before that November day of 1882 when I met you in New Mexico," he often told me, "Sir Walter Scott was perhaps my favorite author. His stories of *Rob Roy* and other heroes, who seemed to spend their lives traveling and having thrilling adventures, made life on a Kentucky farm of the fifties seem almost unbearably tame. I really began to suffer what we called the Western fever...."

He was a tall, muscular youth of seventeen at this time, living on his grandfather's farm near Maysville, in Mason County, Kentucky. There was hard work enough on the farm to make Sir Walter Scott and the other favorite authors of John William (I always called my husband John William, and you must read of him, here, under that name) rainy-day relaxations, for the most part.

"We read—my friends the Matheson boys and I—chiefly on rainy days, when tobacco could not be stripped, nor any farm work carried on. Then

we spent our holiday sprawled on the hay in
Grandfather Poe's barn."

But, John William being the man he was, I
doubt if he could have escaped his attack of
"Western fever" if those old pirated editions of
Scott had never reached Kentucky. By his own
admissions, he owned two ambitions from his
earliest years: he wanted to see the world, and
he wanted to be a financier.

During our married life of nearly forty years
John William told me from time to time more
about his boyhood, and how he came to "hit the
Western trail" at the tender age of seventeen.

These reminiscences I want to bring together
in this chapter. Although I cannot use his own
words, I shall try to give these incidents and
experiences substantially as they came from his
own lips. They form a needful background for the
later chapters, presenting a career as a law-en-
forcement officer that became crowded with
interest and thrills, as the years passed. John
William Poe chose to devote the best years of his
manhood to the cause of law and order in West
Texas and eastern New Mexico when those new
sections were struggling for stability of life and
property.

In all the activities and interests of childhood
and youth on a large Kentucky farm, John
William first displayed that intense energy which
characterized him in later years. Even in its
earlier stages, his life had in it nothing of "half-
measures." If he were following the trail of a

'possum with Stephen Matheson and his brother Judson, or hunting rabbits that hid under the snow-covered weeds which filled the corners of the stake-and-rider fence, he concentrated upon that. If he were practicing on his violin (he had a natural aptitude, and played well by ear) he did it with an almost relentless determination.

But there was a practical motive in these things he did. In boyhood he dreamed of the time when he could escape from the farm and go out into the world upon the adventure of life. It was this thought which gave impetus to everything he did. Even his determination to master the "fiddle" was actuated by the fact that it offered a means of earning money by playing at the country dances—and an accumulation of money was a first requirement of emancipation from the narrow confines of Kentucky.

It was the custom for the young people of the district to gather on Saturday nights in the small brick schoolhouse, and dance away the long winter evenings until the Sabbath sun rose. John William and the Mathesons found a profitable source of income in furnishing the music for these dances. Each dollar that John William received went into the old cowhide trunk brought across the Atlantic by some Irish forbear. This trunk, which stood in a corner of his attic bedroom, was his "treasury."

When he and the Matheson boys had enough money, they would go West. And at last that day came. Covington, forty miles away, was their chosen "jump-off." There a river boat could be boarded for St. Louis.

On the appointed night the three boys slipped quietly out of their windows and started afoot. But while they waited in Covington for the "St. Louis boat" a motherly tavern-keeper persuaded them not to run away. She painted the distress of their families so vividly that the three—homesick, now—went back.

But John William was only delayed, not halted. He continued to save. He was "going West" eventually. He knew it! So he studied the sailing schedules and prices of tickets on the various river boats plying the Ohio River between his home town of Maysville and Cincinnati. He learned that travel by boat was the least expensive, but that he must make every penny count.

He realized the futility of any encouragement from his grandparents in his desires.

"You'll just go to the dogs!" his grandfather snapped at him whenever John William talked of going out to make his own way in life.

The old gentleman wanted his grandson to go to college, at his expense.

"That's the way for a boy of a family like yours to make his start in life. This running off on a wild-goose chase is silly."

John William's father was no more sympathetic. But neither father nor grandfather could persuade the boy to try college. In fact, their arguments only increased his determination to go West.

When the spring of 1870 came and the negroes were again hoeing the long rows of thick, green-leaved tobacco, John William felt that then was the time to escape from the routine of the farm. He felt that there was but one thing to do—he must go!

So one night he again climbed down the ladder from his room window, and again stole away in the night. This time, however, he had but one companion—a cousin named Munson L. Harvey, who likewise had found work on a Kentucky farm depressing. The long forty-mile walk that confronted them was not depressing. They were lucky enough to get several short "lifts" from farmers going to market. But John William did not risk again a change of heart under the influence of the persuasive landlady at the tavern. He gave that place a wide berth, and he and his companion sought lodging elsewhere.

By July 1 the two adventurers were comfortably located not far from Kansas City, where a cousin of John William—Marion Harber—owned a fine farm. The two boys had been unable to resist making this a stopping point in their westward progress. The fascination of the wide fields, with their great crop of wheat ready to be gathered into golden sheaves, had won them to remaining awhile and helping with the harvest.

There was a very practical point involved—the trip had been expensive. They needed more money before they could proceed farther toward the real West.

Notwithstanding the blistering sun, John William worked steadily behind the harvester. He also had to endure all the hardships of a new country. In addition to working in overflows from the Missouri River—which the Indians had named "The Father of Muddy Waters"—he fell a victim to chills and fever early in his Missouri stay and was forced to stop work for about three weeks.

By the time he was well again he decided that he was done with Missouri. He made his plans to push on westward. His cousin, Munson Harvey, had also been a victim of chills, and with his recovery he wanted to leave the region. But his one desire was to return to Kentucky. His longings for adventure had been wholly satisfied; he suffered a bad attack of homesickness.

Munson Harvey's desertion did not influence John William to go back. He paid Munson the seven dollars he owed him and shook his head when the other suggested that they go home together.

"Not for me! I'm going on. I've planned this for as long as I can remember. I'm not going to back out now. You give my love to everybody. Goodbye."

"Well," Harvey said as he climbed aboard the train, "hurry up and make that big killing you're always talking about, and don't wait until you're an old man to come home a millionaire!"

John William left the station with plenty of determination, but with only fifty cents in his pocket. He went at once to his room in a small hotel on a side street and began to pack his few belongings in a small traveling bag. He made an early start the following morning and on foot crossed from Missouri into Kansas. As he walked along, wondering what the first opportunity for work would be, he fell in with a man who was likewise journeying afoot.

From this chance acquaintance he learned that a Frenchman named La Rue, who was farming about three miles from the state line, was in need of a hand. And John William went to La Rue's.

"Well, what kind of work you can do—eh?" Jacques La Rue demanded, resting one leg on the doorstep and wiping the sweat from his heavy face.

"Well," John William responded, "seeing that I'm broke, I'll take any job you can offer. What will you pay?"

"I pay you eighteen dollar for ze month, with ze board and ze room," La Rue said calculatingly.

And thus was a bargain struck on a cold, frosty morning in late September. John William soon found himself digging potatoes in the big patch at the rear of the barn.

As he was giving the spade an extra push with his foot, he heard a commotion behind him. Looking up, he saw old La Rue trip over a hoe handle and fall in his pursuit of a fleeing hen. John William laughed as the Frenchman got up swearing that he "would kill ze damn' hen; she scratch all my hay."

Mrs. La Rue heard the commotion, and turned her motherly eye upon John William. What attracted her instantly was the battered and bruised condition of the boy's hands.

"Why you no wear ze glove for your work?" she cried. "Look at zose hands. *Non! Non!* Zat will not do."

"But I have no money to buy gloves," John William told her.

Muttering in French, the motherly Mrs. La Rue waddled into the kitchen and presently reappeared with a bottle of glycerine and some melted mutton suet. She applied the lotion gently to John William's excruciatingly sore hands, and concluded the treatment with the remark:

"You shall have ze money for ze glove right away."

To her husband she issued an order:

"Look, Jacques, thees boy's hand zey are terribly sore. Give heem money to buy ze glove with—and no hard work until zose hand are better."

Deeply touched by the old lady's solicitude, John William made the simple remark:

"I'll never forget your kindness, Mrs. La Rue," a promise he faithfully kept, for in his later life he took more pleasure in recounting this incident than any of his other Kansas experiences.

Eventually word came to John William from a friend in Kansas City that the Santa Fé Railroad, then under construction, wanted more work hands. The pay was described as on a most liberal scale. That particular point attracted the attention of John William, for he knew that without money his situation was hopeless. The meager returns for his work at La Rue's would not greatly further his westward plans. Although the interest that the La Rues had taken in him, especially Mrs. La Rue's motherly attitude, had endeared them to John William, nevertheless he felt that his best interest required his departure. So after bidding the La Rues a warm goodbye, he picked up his small leather bag again and went on west.

When he reached the Santa Fé construction camp, he found it an easy task for an able-bodied young man to obtain a job. The returns were four dollars a day—a large sum as wages went in those days. But Boss Murphy had a fat contract, and was anxious to push it to completion. He was a hard taskmaster, whipping up by words his construction crew to the utmost.

> *"P'int ahead and cinter back,*
> *And Johnny go and ile th' car."*

Boss Murphy was forever shouting to the crew in his charge, as the men threw the long steel rails of the Santa Fé into place. Then he would add, his Irish brogue asserting itself:

"Heave, there, ye lazy spalpeens! Do yez think ut's a game av croquet ye're playing?" And as he bellowed his commands and comments, the head of the "Big Boss" weaved back and forth as if in time to a railroad chantey.

Then turning to the tall youngster of seventeen, who had not long been a member of the crew, he would grow genial and remark:

"Sure and ut's yersilf is the best worker av thim

all, Johnny Poe. And so I'm giving yez the job av filling the wather tank av the injine afther supper. Ye'll git double pay for ut, because ut's overtime, and yez like the feel av money in yer hand, so Oi've noticed."

It was little wonder that the boss was inclined to favor John William, who had discovered the weakness of this drink-loving Irishman. He assumed a sort of protectorate over Murphy when, after work hours, the older man proceeded to "liquor up." When this had been thoroughly done, John William was usually at hand.

"Just lean on me, Mr. Murphy," he would say. "I'll help you to bed."

Then, without waiting for Murphy's agreement, John William would almost drag his boss into the red boxcar which was bunkhouse for employer and employee alike.

It was a rough life, enlivened by drinking, gambling, and fighting. The boss himself usually took the lead in it all; but John William kept himself clear of the construction crew's "pleasures." His grandfather's prediction in the past, when the "westward progress" was under consideration: "You'll go to the dogs; you're too young to stand out against the temptations of that rough life" only served to strengthen John William's resistance. He would show them all that he had a will of his own.

When not working, John William spent the greater part of his time in the old boxcar reading the newspapers and books supplied by the Santa Fé. There was no common ground on which he could associate with the others he met. They were laborers with no interest in improving themselves.

There was another, and very practical, reason for his determination to neither drink nor gamble. He was working to get money for his travels, and liquor and cards were expensive.

The passing months did not lessen his recurrent attacks of homesickness. His program for himself included a visit to Kentucky as soon as his savings would permit. So he clung to the job until the following autumn, his purse becoming heavier and heavier with the savings from each pay envelope. When he received his last wages, after having given the boss notice that he was quitting, Murphy bestowed a "Good luck to yez, me boy. Ut's a fine lad yez are, and if yez come back there's a job a-waiting f'r yez."

John William stopped in Kansas City long enough to outfit himself with new clothing. And when he got into his bed that night in a modest hotel, he could tell himself with satisfaction that he possessed three hundred dollars. Not only was this a large sum, but it was proof that he had *not* "gone to the dogs" as his grandfather had predicted.

Although he had been away twelve months, John William found everything on the farm of his grandparents just as when he had left. But he himself had changed, and in the course of time he had to admit it to himself. The old homestead was just the same; but John William was not.

Having once escaped from the restricting influence of home, and having undergone enlarge-

ment of mind, body, and character in the great
West that was then in its making, he could no
longer endure being cramped and confined.

So, after a stay of three months in Kentucky,
John William returned to Kansas. He hunted up
Boss Murphy immediately, and found a job with
the same construction crew, then in Topeka.

In the crew was a young man named Dan Hudson, about the age of John William, and between the
two there sprang up a friendship. Dan had been
knocking about in Texas for some time, experiencing many phases of the romantic life to be found
there. He pictured these to his new companion in
glowing colors.

"But western Texas is the hunter's paradise,
so a man told me," Dan Hudson would tell John
William. "Why, there are thousands and thousands
of buffalo roaming the country, like great herds of
cattle. The wolves and deer are so thick you can
kill 'em with a stick. And there are Indians out on
those plains, and anybody who goes out there will
have to fight them. I've heard of more than one
attack on wagon trains where they killed everybody—even the women and children. Those Comanches are savages. Come on, let's go out there.
We can make a big killing when it comes to money,
once we get there."

The enthusiasm of this tall, energetic young
fellow was contagious. John William "caught the
fever" immediately.

"It's just what I've been wanting to do all my
life," he told Dan. "Ever since I was a little shaver,

and my grandfather read the *Leatherstocking Tales* to me, I've wanted to live on the frontier—be a part of it. I'm not worried about dangers—Indians or whatever else may be out there."

And so the two friends made their plans. Together, they would turn their faces toward the "Farther West." They would let nothing stop them.

Before they started, these two young pioneers (for pioneers they were in spirit and fact) equipped themselves with what seemed needed. First on the list was transportation. John William had to invest in a horse. Dan already owned one, and so escaped this item of expense. The purchase made a large hole in John William's savings; but it had to be. There was only eighty dollars left in the small wallet he buttoned inside his gray flannel shirt, when he and his partner started on their eight-hundred-mile journey to the great plains of western Texas, which were then regarded as far beyond the bounds of civilization.

Fort Griffin was their destination. As they skirted the Indian Territory they encountered grim reminders of the lurking danger in the skeletons that occasionally lay bleaching in the sun by the roadside. This was the residue of others who had likewise longed for a share in the conquest of the West, but who had fallen victims to the Indian's resentment of trespassers on his hunting ground.

John William could not help wondering whether he, too, was to become a luckless adventurer, or if the fickle goddess would smile on his efforts.

On the Texas Frontier

IF A LINE WERE RUN due west in Texas from Fort Worth to Albany (county seat of Shackelford), then turned at a right angle and continued northward a few miles to a point near the border of Throckmorton County, it would lead to what remains of old Fort Griffin, located on the Clear Fork of the Brazos River.

In the decade 1870 to 1880, the town was not only notorious as an exemplar of early life in the "Wild West," but it was also notable for its strategic position. It had first attained business importance as a supply depot for the chuck wagons of the Texas cattlemen, who drove their herds up the great overland trail from the southern part of the state. Here, on the trek to Kansan points on the railroad, the drovers halted to take on supplies before continuing up the trail with their herds. Naturally the cowboys sought the kind of relaxation and diversion usual to frontier towns of those times.

The importance of Fort Griffin was increased about 1870 when it became the center of commercialized buffalo hunting, then beginning to extend from Kansas into the plains of West Texas.

All at once the West had realized that there was money in buffalo hides. Scores—hundreds—went into it. During the first stages the hunters kept rather close to the settlements along the newly built railroad in Kansas. The Indian menace kept those early hunters from going farther south into territory which belonged to the red men. The Medicine Lodge Treaty with the Indians stipulated that white hunters should not cross the Arkansas River, all the country below being regarded as reserved for the Indians.

The buffalo hunters, however, had not regarded this deadline, and soon slipped below it. Those who ventured first into the Indian reserves came back to Dodge City, Kansas, bringing such enormous quantities of buffalo hides and telling such alluring stories of the immense numbers of the animals on the plains of Texas, that others were fired with a determination to invade the forbidden territory, and to hunt farther south, despite the risk of Indian encounters.

The long haul to Dodge City, however, proved a drawback to hunting in Texas; but this difficulty was obviated when the firms principally engaged in buying and shipping buffalo hides hastened to establish themselves conveniently for the hunters, who demanded the best in firearms, powder, and lead, as well as food. The natural center of this development was Fort Griffin; and the going and coming of the buffalo hunters, the bringing in of hides from their camps in the creaking wagons, the shipping of them eastward to Fort Worth, gave a distinctive tone to the town for several years, making it unlike almost any other place on the frontier.

Another important feature of the place must

not be overlooked. The United States government
had previously recognized the military importance
of the locality, and upon a large hill above the town
had established the fort itself. During the years
from 1870 to 1880, six or seven companies (a rather
large quota of troops for a frontier post) were stationed there. In addition to officers and private
soldiers, this military establishment contributed
another feature to the miscellaneous assortment of
human beings congregated at Fort Griffin in the
Tonkawa Indian Scouts, commanded by Chief
Johnson. Some of the "Tonks" usually accompanied
the detachments of troops sent after raiding
Comanches.

All of these colorful ingredients tended to make
the town—locally called "The Flat" because of its
location on the level stretch between the hill on
which was located the fort, and the creek below—as
remarkable a collection of rude buildings and rough
inhabitants as ever the West exhibited.

The one long street began at the foot of "Government Hill" and passed in a straight line to the
crossing on the Clear Fork. From end to end, on
both sides, the street was walled with saloons,
gambling dens, dance halls and supply stores, with
a frontage of horses, wagons, ox teams, and bull
trains, all jammed together like *sampans* on the
banks of a Chinese river. Along the plank side-
walks flowed a colorful stream of humanity—
buffalo hunters, cowboys, teamsters—in quest of
what it deemed amusement. These pleasure hunters
usually fell prey to gamblers and dance hall girls.

Mixed with these were soldiers from the fort, likewise in search of relief from the monotonous existence of an isolated army post.

It was into this hotbed of lawlessness and wildness called Fort Griffin that John William and his companion, Dan Hudson, drifted in the spring of 1872. They had ridden many miles through the desert plain of the Texas Panhandle, and then had come into all the excitement that was Fort Griffin. It was no easy thing to resist the seductive temptations of the place—gambling, drinking and women —but John William had developed enough resistance to avoid being lured by any of the frontier viciousness which surrounded him on every hand.

For a brief while he looked on with the interest of an outsider who had spent his life in saner surroundings. But he was not long in this almost insane place before becoming sickened by it. It was not the drinking and the gambling—while instinctively he avoided both liquor and cards, he was not particularly troubled by their presence. But when almost daily he saw a killing over a card game or the favors of some dance hall "queen," he became thoroughly disgusted with Fort Griffin.

Dan Hudson, on the contrary, liked the wild hurly-burly. He decided to stay. So the partnership begun in Kansas was dissolved in Texas.

John William hoped he might get into the buffalo-hunting game, but did not feel that the time was ripe. He was again singlehanded, now that Dan Hudson had chosen the "comforts" of Fort Griffin to the hardships of pushing into the unsettled parts beyond the town. He felt that for a while he must make a living at something else than buffalo hunting.

As he turned his back on Fort Griffin, he little thought that Fate was guiding him toward something more precious than money—a lifelong friend, who would become an important factor in his success during the West Texas period of his life.

Two days later, after a hard ride through the heat of a long May day, John William came to the Barton ranch and stopped to rest, and water his horse. Jim Barton was sitting in the shade of his new plank house, situated on Sweetwater Creek. His long, angular body, square, unshaven jaw, disheveled hair, all bespoke the pioneer. But the hearty greeting he gave John William: "Hello, stranger! Get off and rest your saddle a spell. Kind of hot today, ain't it?" indicated that he was one of those characters who made Texas famous for hospitality.

When John William explained that he was looking for work, Barton immediately offered him a job on his ranch, and John William as promptly accepted.

A few days later, when they sat resting, Barton asked:

"Didn't you say you hailed from Kentucky?"

John William said that Kentucky was his native state and added: "Are you from Kentucky, too?"

"No," Barton replied, "I am Texas, pure Texas. But there's a feller over on Clear Fork, by the name

of Jacobs, who came from Kentucky, too. I just
thought you might like to know. Thought you might
like to get acquainted with him sometime. We call
him John Jay for short."

"I certainly would," John William replied
quickly. "I wonder what's the best time to find him
at home?"

"You can ride over Sunday just as well as not,"
Barton told him. "Likely he'll be there."

So on the following Sunday afternoon, John
William rode off to meet John Jacobs, likewise from
Kentucky, there to begin a friendship that lasted
a lifetime.

Jacobs was resting, for he was completely tired
out by the long week's work of directing "Ben" and
"Lep," the slow-moving oxen that pulled the drag
he was using to get his hundred and sixty acres of
"preëmpted" land under cultivation. He was sitting comfortably on a soapbox behind the rough
little shack he called home, when John William rode
up and said "Howdy!"

"Howdy," Jacobs replied. "Get down and take
a nice soapbox. I'm certainly glad to see another
human. Haven't seen anybody for a whole week."

John William got off his horse and came forward with extended hand.

"I'm John William Poe, lately of Kentucky. I
work for Jim Barton over on the other side of the
creek. He told me you were from Kentucky, too, so
I just rode over to get acquainted."

"Well, I'm certainly glad you did!" Jacobs said
heartily. "My name's John C. Jacobs, but every-

body in these parts calls me John Jay for short.
From Kentucky, too, are you? Well, sir, I'm so
glad to meet somebody from the old Blue Grass
State that if you was a certain golden-haired girl
I know back there, I'd kiss you!"

John William laughed and took the soapbox
Jacobs offered him. They talked the afternoon
away and the more they talked the better they liked
each other.

Jacobs showed the visitor around his farm, and
John William at last made a proposal:

"How about taking me in as a partner? You've
got the land here, and your ox team, and you've
made a good start toward putting in your corn. I
can put in my horse Pete and eighty dollars in cash.
With two of us working, the crop will go in faster,
and it won't be so lonesome, either."

"I could take you in as a partner," Jacobs said
hesitantly, "where I couldn't afford to hire you. If
you want to risk paying yourself out of our corn
crop, I'll certainly do my part to see that we both
get paid off."

They shook hands on the deal, and John William
went back to tell Jim Barton he was moving over
to Jacobs' place.

That was the beginning of a partnership which
was to continue through frontier dangers and
trials, and of a friendship which would last as long
as the two men lived.

Both were farmers. Both were young, strong,
energetic and—very important on a pioneer homestead—ingenious. They became masters of make-

shift. In order that more and quicker planting might be accomplished, they improvised single harness for Jacobs' oxen. John William could plow, while Jacobs followed with the other ox, harrowing.

They came to know each other very well during the long evenings when the lumbering oxen had been corralled behind the shack. Then, over their pipes, the two young men talked of their past and of plans for the future.

John William's determination to accumulate money was as strong as when he left Kentucky. Often he would take out his pocketbook and count the precious bills for which he had worked so hard. Jacobs laughed good-naturedly at his partner's financial ambitions.

He was not so much interested in saving money as in enjoying life. But there was a golden-haired girl back in Kentucky whom he wanted to marry. He told John William all about her, and of his reasons for leaving Kentucky and coming to Texas. Money had always slipped through his fingers, spent easily for good clothes, and dancing, and entertaining girls. It was to escape temptation to spend his money that he had come down to this Texas farm.

When he looked out over their wide cornfield he pictured the time when it would be harvested and sold and he, with a full wallet, could return to his home state and marry the girl. That was his only reason for wanting money.

The corn grew fast and strong from that virgin

soil. On a day when it was beginning to tassel, John William looked at it and suggested a holiday.

"It looks like it's growing a foot a day," he told Jacobs. "I think we can leave it alone for awhile. Sowbelly is getting pretty monotonous. Let's go hunting and get some fresh meat."

Jacobs was staring at the sky and when he spoke his remark had no bearing on hunting.

"What the hell's that?" he grunted. "There's not a cloud in the sky, but look at that haze in the east!"

"Maybe it's an eclipse of the sun," John William told him lightly, without interest. "We wouldn't know! Out here, we don't even know what day of the week it is."

But they stood staring at that haze which swiftly moved across the sky. Quickly an enormous green cloud was over them, and from the cloud came a metallic buzzing that seemed to fill all the air about them. They looked at each other.

"*Grasshoppers!*" they said hopelessly. "There goes our corn!"

The enormous swarm of grasshoppers descended upon the field. By four o'clock that afternoon, not a blade of grass was on the ground, not a leaf was on a tree, not a stalk of corn was left in the field. Their farm was as bare and brown as a desert. They stood outside their little shack and looked all around. Jacobs shrugged.

"And there goes my wedding! John William, let's hit the trail away from this damn' place. You wanted to go hunting. All right! Here's our chance to take a long spell of it. We'll sell the oxen, and I'll buy a horse."

John William agreed instantly. There was no profit to be made on the farm that year.

"They're paying a dollar apiece for wolf pelts, over at Fort Griffin," he told Jacobs. "Let's get out in the timber and try our luck. We might make as much that way as in farming. Anyway, we've got to do something."

So the oxen were sold, and a pony bought for Jacobs with the proceeds. Then, with their meager belongings in two saddlepacks, the two Johns started for the hunting grounds.

"I wouldn't bother even to lock the door of the old shack," Jacobs told John William, who was taking a last look at the inside. "Any man who's damn' fool enough to want the place can have it with my compliments."

But this irritation wore off presently. Some months later he returned and sold the place, using the money to buy ammunition and guns for the partners' buffalo hunt.

"We'd better get away out in the timber where there are not so many hunters, if we expect to kill wolves by the wholesale. They've been hunted so much right around here that they won't let you come within shooting distance," John William remarked as they rode westward.

Several days later the two young men decided to make camp near a thicket of post oaks, in the midst of which they could hope to be unnoticed by any Comanches who might be roaming the plains.

This became their permanent camp, and the hunting began. Each day was divided between killing the wolves and skinning them. Wolves were numerous enough and, when at sundown they quit the day's work, they always had a pile of green pelts to stake.

Several months drifted by. When October came, the nights grew much too cold for their light bedding. One morning, John William, waking after a frosty night that had chilled him to the very bones, told Jacobs it was time to move:

"What do you say to calling off the hunt? We've been out here, now, for six months. I'm tired of having just you to look at, and maybe you're feeling the same about me. For a change, I think I'd even like to mingle with that herd around Fort Griffin—tough as they are. We can get some news from outside, too. How many pelts have we got?"

"About four hundred and eighty-nine, if I haven't missed the count," Jacobs answered. "And now that you mention it, I think I *would* like some different company, myself! Afraid we're getting kind of stale, living out here by ourselves. Besides, winter'll be here soon, according to the way it feels this morning. Let's rattle our hocks back to the settlement, as soon as Nigger Charlie comes out with the wagon to take the pelts in. You know, I reckon we've made about as much as we would if we'd stayed on that grasshopper-eaten claim."

When the negro teamster, Charlie Fowler, came out with his wagon, the two young hunters broke camp and returned to Fort Griffin The pelts were sold at the government commissary for $489, which seemed almost a fortune to the hunters. It was a proud moment for the partners when they walked into the store of Conrad & Rath—general supply merchants and bankers for all that section around Fort Griffin—and deposited, each his half, this amount to their separate accounts.

While the boys were loafing around the fort, the commandant sent for them. He made the proposition that they contract to supply fuel for the post during the following winter. Though they knew it would mean plenty of hard work, the two Johns signed a contract to furnish sixteen hundred cords of wood at a price of one dollar a cord. Again they thought they saw a fortune coming toward them.

As they were leaving the government commissary after completing the signing of the contract, John William said to his partner:

"You know, those grasshoppers begin to look to me like a blessing in disguise! If it hadn't been for them, we'd still be walking behind those old steers, up and down the furrows. As it is, now we can afford to buy a few things; we can be comfortable while we're out after this wood. Suppose you go down to the store and get us a couple of government blankets, while I go and see Negro Charlie about hauling our camp stuff out. And, while you're buying, better get a new skillet, and a couple of good butcher knives, and some tin cups."

With this new stock of supplies loaded in Negro Charlie's wagon, they rode toward the heavy timber some thirty miles south of Fort Griffin. When they reached what seemed a place safe from the view of passing bands of Indians, they unloaded their equipment and pitched camp. Negro Charlie, having completed his part in establishing the wood-cutters at their work, turned back for the settlement. So John William and Jacobs were once again by themselves.

That evening, after the partners had finished their supper of sourdough bread and sowbelly and strong coffee, John William said:

"We'd better put out that fire. You know those bloodthirsty Comanches are always on the lookout for small camps like ours. I'll go hide the ponies in that shin-oak thicket while you stamp out the coals. What's more, we ought to make our beds in a different place each night."

And these precautions were a part of the regular evening routine during all their stay in that locality.

One bright moonlight night, some weeks later, John William suddenly jumped to his feet with a cry of pain, and began stamping the ground vigorously where he had been lying asleep in his blankets. Jacobs, roused from sound sleep, sat up quickly.

"What's the matter?" he cried. "Indians?"

Without answering the question, John William exploded:

"For God's sake get the soda, quick! I've been stung by a centipede at the back of my neck. Hurry up!"

Jacobs flung his blankets aside and jumped up. He scratched hurriedly around among the pots and pans in quest of the can of soda, but found the whisky bottle first. He had the frontiersman's faith in whisky as a panacea for all human ills. So he uncorked the bottle and ran with it to John William who, by this time, was nearly delirious with pain. Into a tin cup Jacobs poured a big drink and John William gulped it.

As he helped his stricken companion to lie down again in his blankets, Jacobs saw the remains of the huge, loathsome insect which had bitten John William.

Not content with the whisky, Jacobs made a soda poultice and applied it to the bitten spot. Then he folded his own blanket so as to make a cushion and at the foot of a post oak proceeded to keep vigil through the rest of the night. At short intervals he renewed the poultice, while John William groaned with pain.

For several days John William's life hung in the balance. Or Jacobs thought so. He lay under the shade of a wagon sheet which was stretched over an oak pole, which served as their camp house and shelter from rain. He was too ill to move, with that terrible pain in the back of his head. All the time, Jacobs nursed him faithfully. There can be no doubt that it was this careful tending, coupled with John William's robust constitution, which finally brought about his recovery.

The nearest water to this camp was three miles away. Whenever Negro Charlie came out to haul a load of wood back to the post, he brought along a barrel of water. Once a week, the pair walked the three miles to the spring and enjoyed a drink of the fresh water. The time for these trips would be on Saturday night, this being chosen, not because the following day was Sunday, but because the ways of civilization would reassert themselves even on the frontier. Saturday night remained associated in their minds with a, then, extraordinary use of water.

This visit to the spring had to be made cautiously. As it was the only spring in the vicinity, there was always danger that Indians might at any time be lurking near by.

Each of them averaged three cords of wood a day at their cutting. The days drifted into weeks, the weeks into months. The partners had been all the while engaged in chopping and cording wood. Cowboys on near-by ranches voted them "queer" because, as they said, "them fellows keep plugging away like water wearing away a granite cañon wall." What further added to their peculiarities in the cowboy mind, was the fact that the two never stopped their work even to attend a dance.

The late fall days came, and when the leaves began to turn from golden brown to deep red in the autumn sun, the two wood choppers had stacked the last of their sixteen hundred cords. At the close of the final day's work, John William threw his battered, sweaty hat high in the air, and whooped like an Indian.

"We can sleep, tomorrow! For we've got sixteen hundred dollars coming from Uncle Sam."

But that program—to sleep late—was not carried out. Just at nightfall, a notorious character named Bill Whittaker rode over from one of the ranches. He was not a welcome visitor, for he was considered an old profligate. In the back of that buckboard in which he made his trips about the country was always a jug of corn whisky. He pulled in at the woodcutters' camp with a broad grin.

"Heard that you young fellows had finished your contract. Thought maybe you'd like to celebrate. I figured you wouldn't want to do it by yourselves, so I stopped at Barton's ranch and give the boys there an invite."

The surprise party was a "howling" success. Under the influence of good fellowship—and Bill Whittaker's jug—John William "broke over" for the first time. Starting with one drink, on the theory that on a festive occasion one drink, more or less, makes no difference, he embarked upon a series in which one led to another—and yet another, until, the festivities over, he was in a condition in which, as he himself afterward expressed it: "the ground came up and slapped me in the face."

Jacobs had not been roused from his usual indifference to whisky. When the last cowboy had departed, he drew the blanket over his partner and turned in peacefully.

When daylight came Jacobs found his partner "far from himself." So he dosed him with strong coffee. Then, as he waited for this to have its effect, he packed up their camp equipment, preparatory to starting back to Fort Griffin. When John William came to himself, he was filled with disgust at having succumbed to a phase of frontier life which he utterly loathed.

"Never again, so help me," he exclaimed, "will I ever allow myself to drink enough to get drunk."

And only once did he break that resolution.

Their return to Fort Griffin created something of a sensation. As they drove down the street toward the commissary, whom should they meet but Joe McCombs, one of their associates in the farming days.

"Hello, you God-forsaken heathens!" he yelled. "Come back to civilization, did you? Well, I was thinking the other day that, if you didn't come back soon, you'd turn into a couple of them damn' Comanches. Come on down! The drinks are on me."

"Thanks, Joe, but not this time," Jacobs declined for them both. "You know I never touch the stuff, and John William here had enough the other night to last him a good long time; but if you've got anything to chew on besides sowbelly, we're your huckleberries."

"Range of the Buffalo"

WITH THE RETURN to Fort Griffin in 1873, John William felt, more insistently than ever before, the lure of the great buffalo hunt going on over the hundreds of miles of plains, now dotted by such Texas cities as Midland, Plainview, Abilene, and Big Springs. On the street corners, in the rooming houses and eating places—everywhere he turned in Fort Griffin, the sole topic of conversation seemed to be that of buffalo hunting. Everyone talked of buffalo and the "big killing" that was going on. Men spoke of the countless herds roaming the plains, and bragged of the fabulous number of buffalo they had killed.

None seemed to have the least sympathy for the animals themselves or any compunction about their rapid extermination. In fact, all seemed to feel it was the buffalo's fate to become a sacrifice to the advance of civilization.

There were several reasons for this feeling: The cattlemen grumbled about the buffalo's eating all the grass away from their cows. They claimed that cattle could not be raised, so long as the buffalo occupied the country. Others, who wished to see the country rid of the menace of the Indian, argued that the Indian could never be brought under control, so long as there were buffalo, for the buffalo supplied the Indian with everything needful for his living—food, tepee-coverings, clothing, leather for his pony's trappings. They maintained that if the West were ever to be settled by the Whites, the buffalo must go; for as long as they were there, the Indians would rove over their hunting preserves.

In addition to these arguments, tending to seal the doom of this noble animal, there was a third reason—probably even more compelling. Buffalo hides brought from a dollar to three dollars in answer to the demand for robes—although the leather was too porous to be used for shoe leather, it was quickly discovered. Such a demand sent hundreds of eager men out on the buffalo range to do their part in decimating the big herds.

Fort Griffin, just then, was filled with men outfitting. When these hunters were provided with guns, ammunition, provisions, and camping equipment, they departed hastily with creaking, loaded wagons, to spend the winter somewhere on the Great Plains within two hundred miles or so of Fort Griffin. Their camps they hoped to locate advantageously in the path of the buffalo on their southward migration—for the great herds roamed to the north and then returned again to the warmer clime as they willed. Each of these hunters expected to pile up buffalo hides, the profits from which would be almost fabulous.

Very naturally, the two successful woodcutters caught "buffalo fever" and, after a few days of loafing about Fort Griffin, they decided to have a fling at the game. They invested part of their money from the wood contract in a wagonload of supplies—which included not only bedding and provisions enough for several months in the field, but also two of the powerful Sharps rifles known to the hunters as "The Big Fifty," then considered the best buffalo-killing weapon on the market, having a range of a mile or more.

They bought a plentiful supply of powder, lead, and primers, with a complete reloading outfit. They also engaged the services of Joe McCombs, whose double office was to skin the buffalo that were killed, and to play the role of professional jester. Joe remained with them during the several years they were hunting, and whiled away much of the loneliness and tedium of their isolated life by his pranks and witticisms.

When the party of three drove away from Fort Griffin, they were determined to amass a big stake on the buffalo range. At Paint Creek, sixty-five miles from Fort Griffin, they made their first camp. Here they remained for two months, and their stay was well rewarded, for during that period they killed four hundred buffalo.

But other hunters, hearing of the luck of the Poe-Jacobs outfit, and that buffalo were more plentiful where they were camped, came flocking there, until they crowded the two Johns too closely for comfort. So the Poe-Jacobs outfit moved farther out, and tried their luck for the balance of the season in an entirely different territory.

When they had accumulated a large number of hides, it seemed best for Jacobs to haul them in to

Fort Griffin and dispose of them. While he was on this trip, John William and McCombs were to take the wagon with the camp paraphernalia, and locate a new camping spot, which they planned to make some two hundred miles farther to the west. The location they had in mind was in the vicinity of the old Phantom Hill military post. It had been so long abandoned by the army that nothing remained to mark the spot but several ghostly looking stone chimneys. These served as a landmark for the nomadic buffalo hunters.

Before Jacobs left for Fort Griffin, a question rose: How was he to trail the outfit, after it had gone ahead into what was truly a pathless wilderness? John William evolved a novel scheme which, in after years, he liked to describe. The understanding was that when John William had traveled an estimated fifty miles he was to drive a stake into the ground. As roving Indians might destroy any note of directions that might be attached to the stake, he was to step off thirty paces to the right, and at that point bury a tomato can containing whatever written instructions he might wish to convey to Jacobs.

In later times Jacobs often described his long, weary drive back from Fort Griffin in the wake of his partner. Walking behind a yoke of plodding oxen, he was all of a week in covering the first fifty miles from the outfit's old campsite, and was uncertain all the time that he was going in the right direction. But when he found the first stake that had been erected, and located the buried tin can with John William's instructions, his depression and doubt vanished.

"I had a feeling," he would say in characteristic fashion, "like a man's when he meets his dear old mother after years of separation. I just wanted to yell like a Comanche, but discretion said I better not, as there might be real Indians prowling around. So, as the oxen were about petered out from the long day's pull, I thought I'd just camp right there and get an early start in the morning, hoping to catch up with John William and Joe next day.

"But I'll be gol-derned if I hadn't lost my matchbox—or left it where I'd camped last time. So I set down and tried to think how I could start a fire. Finally I tore a piece of flour sack into little strips, and unraveled the threads until I had a handful of soft cotton. Then I pulled the bullet from a ca'tridge and mixed the powder with the ravelings. I packed this mixture into an empty shell and piled up a lot of dry grass and shot off the old buffalo gun right into it. And, begorry, I had a fire in short order!

"Then I hobbled out old Tom and Jerry, and while the coffee was boiling I stretched out on the dry grass and went to dreaming about tomorrow and how jolly it would seem to see my pards again. It was sure lonesome, sleeping out every night, with just the stars for company. I was sort of dozing off, I reckon, when suddenly I heard footsteps. It was too dark to see more'n ten foot away, so I grabbed the old six-shooter—thinking I'd die fighting, anyway—and then I heard Joe's old familiar laugh. Say, it sounded sweeter than any gal's laugh to me, just then!

" 'Well, we heard your shot, and we thought maybe it was you, trying to signal us. So we came right along to let you know you was on the right trail,' Joe told me.

"And I was sure glad to see them boys. Nothing will get a man more'n being alone out on the plains. Something about it's kind of spooky, especially at night."

"The boys" stirred up the fire, and put on more buffalo chips so that they could look at each other. Then John William sat down and began to question his partner about the trip.

Jacobs reported the news of Fort Griffin, as well as all the incidents occurring on his long trip, then the others told him of the big herds of buffalo they had seen and the prospects of good hunting.

Early the next morning after this reunion, the three adventurers pushed on. For several days they forced their way into the wilderness. At the end of another week they agreed on a campsite in a clump of scrubby brush under a steep knoll. Here, John William decided, was the best place for a permanent winter camp; but prior to that, they would have to do some big killing, as their tepee was to be constructed of buffalo hides.

Buffalo were so numerous that they had not far to go to make a "big killing." But Joe McCombs' mind was running in another direction from that of buffalo. For herds of wild horses ranged within a few miles of the camp, and Joe's heart was set on owning a particular black stallion which he called "Jim Grilliky."

"I tell you, boys, he's the finest hoss I ever put eyes on, and I'm a-going to get him," Joe would tell the others.

Joe's method of capture was an old trick used on the frontier to capture wild horses. The method was known as "creasing." Just back of a horse's head is a nerve, which, if penetrated by a bullet, will produce temporary paralysis. An expert marksman can sometimes fell a horse in this manner. Capture thereafter is a comparatively easy matter —but the marksman has to be an expert shot.

"I'll get that hoss or bust a hamstring," Joe declared one day as he left camp. "I'll just pick him off with my Sharps, then I'll rope and ride him to a fare-thee-well."

But the long day passed without Joe's return. John William and Jacobs were engrossed in the regular excitement of the hunt, and paid little attention to Joe's delayed return. But about midnight, as they were cooking a late supper, John William cried out:

"Look—look! What's that thing coming through the grass?"

The singular-looking creature came close enough to be recognizable, and Jacobs, unable to keep from laughing, said:

"Well, bless my soul! If it ain't that red-headed horse creaser that left this camp—seems about a week ago—to bring back the finest stallion on the plains. What's the matter, Joe? You look like something that's been run through the hackles of hell. Did the Comanches collect your scalp?"

"You'd *think* it was hell, if you'd been along with me!" Joe told him, as he limped into camp. "You sure missed the sight of your life."

"But where's your breeches, man?" Jacobs interrupted. "Looks like the Comanches scalped the wrong end of you!"

For Joe McCombs was trouserless and, as a full suit of underwear was taboo in Buffalo Land, that meant he was "in the altogether" in respect to his legs, which were scratched and bleeding from their contact with thorns and cactus. His face was sun-blistered and, altogether, Joe was a disreputable-looking object.

He threw himself down by the tepee, and relieved himself with muleskinner freedom.

"If you two —— will stop laughing, I'll tell you what happened," he exploded. "After I left camp, I run right into my 'Jim Grilliky' and his harem, soon as I got out over that there rise to the east. So I begun creeping up closer, all the time keeping to the lee side of the herd, so they couldn't catch my smell. I finally got so near I had to shoot, for they was getting that restless they was likely to stampede any minute. Old 'Jim Grilliky' was throwing his head up and sniffing the breeze, the way a hoss does when he's looking for trouble.

"So I ups and busts loose with my old Sharps charcoal-burner and I sure landed him one right in the neck—just right. He dropped as pretty as any-

thing you ever see, and I burned the breeze getting
to him. And then I found that, like the gol-derned
fool I was, I'd forgot my rope. Hell, but I was dam-
gasted! Well, I had to take my pants off and tear
'em into strips to make a lariat. But I had him tied
hard and fast before he came to, and then I stood
off to watch what he'd do—and I'll be *damned* if he
didn't give one long shiver, and stretch out dead-
er'n a doornail!"

He shook his head miserably.

"And there *I* stood with not a dern thing on but
this dirty old shirt—and four miles from camp!
What with the damn' cactus and catclaw, my legs
feel like they'd been flayed!"

Jacobs swore irritably:

"And what the devil are you going to do now
for pants, you blithering idiot? Do you think maybe there's a store, or a tailor shop, right around the
next bend?"

"Make a pair out of buffalo hide, why don't
you?" John William suggested. "You can have 'the
skinny side out and the woolly side in,' as the old
song goes, 'and the devil go wid yez, sez Brian O'
Lynn!'"

Everybody laughed. And Joe, much cheered,
said:

"I'll do that very thing! They'll do to cover my
legs until I can get back to Fort Griffin."

The next day Joe cut himself a pair of trousers
from a buffalo skin. He selected the softest hide
among the large number on hand; sitting half-
naked on the ground he cut and sewed together a

garment which was both strangely and most wonderfully made!

When Jacobs returned from the day's shooting, he inquired:

"Well, Joe, how's the pants coming along?"

Joe held them up for inspection, and Jacobs grinned.

"Mighty fine, Joe. Just about as good as you'd get at Hamberg's store, out of them Kansas City duds he hauled in last fall."

"Well," Joe decided, after a critical look at his work, "they're a little previous, but I wouldn't mind if it wasn't for the cockleburs and sand in the damn' hair. Makes a fellow feel all the time like ants was crawling up his legs."

However, Joe did not have to put up with the burs and sand for the rest of the winter. During the next week, another hunter happened to stop at the camp, and as he was on his way to Fort Griffin for supplies, he undertook to bring back a pair of trousers for Joe. In the course of time they were received, and Joe was relieved of his buffalo hide pants.

But before this occurred, he met with another misfortune—connected somehow with the garment of buffalo skin. One day while he was preparing the noon meal, he had occasion to go over to the wagon box for corn meal with which to make the daily "pone." Hardly had he thrust his hand into the box than he jumped up into the air and let forth a terrific scream. John William ran to his assistance.

"What in Tophet's the matter with you, Joe?"
he demanded.

"I'm snake-bit!" Joe screamed.

He began to tear the buffalo hide pants off. In
a second or two he stood bare legged, holding one
leg of the pants in each hand and shaking them furiously. Something dropped to the ground which
Joe immediately crunched under his heel.

"There, you damn' stingaree," he yelled. "I'll
teach scorpions to crawl up a man's breeches!"

While these little "pleasantries" helped to re-
lieve the monotony of their daily life, there was always the menace of Indians to keep them constantly watchful. In fact, their nearest neighbors were
a band of Indians only about twenty miles away,
and all those in the Poe-Jacobs outfit realized they
must be constantly on guard against an attack.
Each man kept his cartridge belt constantly filled
and ready for any emergency.

The Indians were not disposed to bother those
who were well provided with a good rifle and plenty
of ammunition; but the man who "took a chance"
out on the plains without this necessary protection,
was always the target for their attacks. The fact
that the buffalo hunters, though usually few in
numbers, were dead shots and always armed to the
teeth and on their guard, served to secure them im-
munity from much Indian trouble.

The Poe-Jacobs camp had its "baptism of fire,"
nonetheless. A few months after they had started
on this first expedition, a band of Comanches escaped from their reservation at Fort Sill and at-

tacked the camp. A few shots from the terrible buffalo guns served to send the Indians running to cover over the sand hills. The soldiers sent on the trail of these runaways soon caught up with them and conducted them back to the reservation. Among them was a young chief who, when questioned about this fight, expressed himself in straightforward pigeon-English:

"Huuh! Me heap no like buffalo gun. Him shoot today, kill tomorrow! Heap bad medicine for Injun!"

Besides gun and ammunition, the buffalo hunters carried several knives for skinning the animals, and a large steel "sharpener" with which to keep the knives in keen condition. The best portions of the meat which the hunters used were the tongue and the hump, with occasionally other choice portions of the carcass; but for the most part the meat was left for the wolves and coyotes.

Though the success of the buffalo-hunting outfit was largely dependent on the marksmanship of the shooter—in this instance both Johns did the killing—yet the skinner (in this outfit Joe McCombs) had much to do with the success of the expedition. A good skinner was an absolute necessity, and the man took just as much pride in his part of the work as did the shooter who brought the animal down, for it required no little skill to remove a hide without slitting or cutting it unnecessarily.

The skinner was usually equipped with a large supply of skinning knives. Some of the hunters carried along a small grindstone with which to keep the edges of their skinning knives in perfect condition. The old Wilson knife was a general favorite in those days among all hunters.

In the opinion of the Poe-Jacobs outfit, the best skinner they ever employed, a man who worked with them on several of their later hunts, was Thomas Kilpatrick. He prided himself on being able to skin from fifty to sixty buffalo a day, without regarding it as an extra heavy day's job.

The best skinners were artists at their work. They would begin cutting at the head, commencing at the under jaw. A long, straight incision would be made from the brisket to the tail. Next, the skinner would rip straight down each fore leg and each hind leg. Then he would proceed to remove the hide, beginning at the jaws. When he had peeled back the hide as far as the backbone on one side, the animal would be turned, and the same process repeated on the other side.

Some hunters, who were in a hurry to remove the hides, and did not take as much pains as others, would fasten a rigging to the skin and the other end to a horse and thus strip off the hide in a hurry. But this method was not resorted to by hunters who desired to bring their hides to market in the best possible condition.

As the skins were heavy, usually the skinner made them into a roll for greater ease in handling. He would spread the whole skin out on the ground, then roll the legs under, making the hide about three feet wide. The roll was completed by beginning at the jaws and rolling down toward the tail. The completed roll was as easily thrown into the wagon as a sack of flour.

After the skins were hauled into camp, the next process was known as "pegging out." It was necessary that the skins be laid in the sun to dry, and for removal of any surplus flesh which the skinner had overlooked. In this part of the work, everyone attached to the outfit took part, no matter what his regular duty might be. A large supply of pegs was always kept on hand. These were about six inches long and an inch in diameter. With these, the hides were pinned out on smooth ground in the vicinity of the camp. The "curing" was done by the sun's rays.

Every buffalo hunter's camp was usually surrounded with scores of hides thus spread out to dry. If the wind and weather were right, a week or ten days saw the hides in good shape for the next step, that of "fleshing." This, as previously stated, consisted in the removal of the surplus flesh with some sort of a scraper. The method which determined readiness of the hides for fleshing was to walk over them several days after they had been pegged out, listening to the "rattle" they made. If this indicated the right degree of dryness, the fleshing was commenced forthwith.

After the hides were properly dried and fleshed, they were stacked in great piles. This process was known as "ricking." When the hides were ready to be hauled to market, this "ricking" was done in its own peculiar way. Each hide was doubled down in the middle with the fur inside. When a number of hides had been made ready in this manner, the "stack" was commenced.

First, a layer of brush was spread, so that the hides would not come in contact with damp ground. On this foundation the folded hides were stacked until the pile attained a height as great as a man could reach. Then an old bull's hide, of little or no market value, would be placed over the pile as a cover, the ends being held down with strips of green hide—or rocks, if available.

The several seasons ending in 1878, during which the Poe-Jacobs outfit was on the buffalo range, represented the peak of the killing of these animals. The traffic in this commodity far exceeded, financially, for the time being, that of either farms or the cattle trail in Texas. The fact that the warehouse of Conrad & Rath, at Fort Griffin, usually contained thirty tons of lead and five tons of powder for the use of the buffalo hunters, serves to show the immense trade in ammunition done by this one firm alone, and suggests the enormous number of buffalo that were killed each season. Other firms, such as York & Draper, William McKenney, and T. E. Jackson were as lavishly provided with ammunition for the hunters.

It was at these stores the hunters gathered between seasons and exchanged their experiences. As they rested up from the strenuous work of killing, skinning and curing buffalo hides during the season, they vied with each other in recounting thrilling tales of experiences that had been theirs—

narrow escapes from wounded buffalo or marauding Indians and the like. Sometimes there were brief tributes to those who had failed to return, having died somewhere out on the range.

The summer was usually spent in laying in new supplies of guns and ammunition; and with each succeeding year the quantity of these supplies that went out with each party of hunters seemed to increase until the peak of the killing was past.

When the warmth and greenness of spring were assuredly at hand, the first season of the Poe-Jacobs outfit might be said to have come officially to an end. John William and Jacobs, with their faithful skinner and camp jester, McCombs, broke camp and drove back to Fort Griffin. They brought with them eleven hundred hides, which they sold for a dollar each. It seemed good to be back among people once more, where they got a thrill out of the presence of their fellow beings, rough as most of them were.

"Why," one of the trio remarked later, "we were thrilled just to see clothes hanging on a line."

And who wouldn't be, after having been completely cut off from civilization for six months?

But as the weeks and months passed, and the cool of autumn again approached, the two hunters grew tired of lounging around the fort. In fact, for such energetic young fellows as John William and Jacobs, any sort of life of ease and inactivity was out of the question. Long before the actual time for starting back to the buffalo range, they were anxious to be off, and John William continually hummed the words of an old range song:

"Come all you jolly fellows, and listen to my song;
There are not many verses, and it won't detain
*   you long;*
It's all about three fellows, who did agree to go
And spend a season pleasantly on the range of
*   the buffalo!"*

And so, when September, 1877, came, the two Johns, with Joe McCombs and a fourth companion, Tom Kilpatrick, found themselves setting out upon another buffalo hunt. This time they pitched camp on the banks of Clearwater River, near the spot now occupied by the town of that name.

One feature of this second season's hunt that made it stand out clearly among them all, was the fact that wild turkeys were numerous in the vicinity. These were no ordinary wild turkeys. They had fattened on the great crop of pecans in that locality, until they were "fit for the palate of an epicure." Often, in relating this circumstance, John William would tell of finding not one tree, but several, along the Clearwater, filled with roosting wild turkeys. A single discharge of a shotgun would bring down half a dozen of the fat birds. This savory addition to the meager, monotonous menu of the hunting camp, or even of the Fort Griffin "hash-houses," made the Clearwater camp a memorable one, even though it failed to come up to their expectations in the number of buffalo found there.

The latter part of September they abandoned the Clearwater location and moved camp farther west to a spot known in those days as "Lone Wolf," later to be the site of Colorado City. Here they found buffalo by thousands. But there were drawbacks to this buffalo hunter's paradise. The water was bad. Joe McCombs grumbled about it constantly, saying he could not get the taste of "that asquinth" out of his mouth if he lived to be as old as Methuselah. Finally, to escape from this unfavorable condition at Lone Wolf, they moved camp to a spot known as Signal Peak.

As everything here seemed thoroughly favorable, they determined to establish themselves for the winter by building a tepee of buffalo hides. The two requirements were: first, that it should be large enough to accommodate the whole party; and second, that it should be built stout enough to serve as a fort. For the walls of the house they used a reinforced construction of nine layers of hides, built to a height well above the head of the tallest of the party. These thicknesses were sufficient to stop any bullet from the most powerful buffalo gun— even if the Indians were able to get hold of one of those weapons. At the apex was the usual opening for the escape of smoke. It was a habitation warm enough for the most rigorous winter weather they might expect, as well as a safe retreat from any attack of prowling redskins.

At Signal Peak they found the hunting so excellent that they added three skinners to the party, while the others did the killing. It was not good policy to kill off the buffalo at a faster rate than the skinners could conveniently do their part of the work. Now, with three more skinners, the total of animals could be greatly increased. And the presence of the added men increased the amount of sociability. John William always recalled pleasantly the life they led in this buffalo hide tepee, particularly the time they spent around the evening fire.

It was by no means all gossip and good-natured chaffing. There was much work for each member of the outfit. For one thing, there were the cartridges which had to be reloaded for the next day's shooting. In that dangerous locality, the buffalo hunter was always very particular about the state of his ammunition, and the amount to be kept on hand for possible emergencies of defense. He took no chances with old ammunition. Every cartridge must be freshly and truly made. So, many of the evenings were spent thus. One cleaned the empty shells and reprimed them; another melted great skillets of lead—often from fifty to eighty pounds at a time being used. A third poured the molten metal into the bullet moulds, while to the most expert ammunition maker was allotted the task of filling the shells with the correct amount of powder and carefully seating the bullet.

If the ammunition supply did not need replenishing, the men spent the time in mending their clothing, which naturally became ragged and torn under the hardships of the hunt. They washed their clothes in a stream of running water. They liked this method, as all they had to do was to tie a shirt to a snag at the edge of the stream and let the water do the rest. It was "Nature's own washing machine," chuckled John William.

Time never dragged in camp. If all else failed, there was always the resourceful Joe McCombs with his "foolishness." His practical jokes were always memorable; but there was one in particular that John William delighted to recount, because it was directed against himself. Joe McCombs had been biding his time to "get back" at John William, for his "hurrahing" about Joe's expedition after the black stallion, and his wearing of the buffalo hide pants.

At length, Joe's opportunity came to even the score. One night he proposed to his comrades that they hold a mock trial. The suggestion met with instant favor. Joe thereupon proceeded to organize the court, appointing himself as "prosecuting attorney," making one of the skinners the "judge," designating Jacobs and the two other skinners as "jury," while John William became the "defendant." The latter was "arraigned" before "His Honor," whose chair of justice consisted of an empty powder can.

The accusation against the prisoner was based on an occurrence of the preceding day. John William had gone out to hunt as usual, but finding the wind unfavorable, had decided to return to camp. As he stopped at a pool for a drink, he had seen a flock of curlews stalking about in the water hole. On impulse he had raised his gun and fired. The birds took wing immediately, and as he watched them disappear, he observed that one of them had the cleaning rod of his rifle imbedded in its body.

John William was disgusted with himself on two counts. He had not killed any of the curlews, and he had lost a favorite cleaning rod. This was the offense charged against him in this mock court, with Joe McCombs as the "prosecuting attorney." All present were expecting great amusement. They knew Joe would have something ridiculous in the way of an "address" to the "jury."

Joe solemnly got to his feet.

"Gentlemen of the jury," he began, conventionally enough, but with a woebegone expression on his face, as he addressed the "jury," who were sitting cross-legged on the ground to the right of the "court." Then, following a long pause, he continued, with the utmost deliberation and solemnity, "I have before Your Honor one John William Poe, the best shot on the plains of Texas; a man who has killed more buffalo than Samson killed Philistines; a man who is without fear of the very devil himself. He is now being tried for murder in the first degree, having shot his cleaning rod into the south end of a poor, defenseless bird without provocation, and with full intent and purpose to commit murder."

When the "prosecuting attorney" had reached this point, there was an interruption of groans and peals of laughter. The groans came from the "jurors," the "judge," and even the prisoner himself, all having been "deeply moved" by the mock-heroics of Joe McCombs. The case was immediately given to the "jury" which, after going aside and conferring a few moments, brought in a verdict of "first degree murder." The "judge" forthwith passed sentence to the effect that John William Poe be sentenced to buy one dollar's worth of chewing tobacco for the "court" (the term being used in a comprehensive and collective sense) at the first opportunity.

The hunters closed this second season with ten thousand hides to their credit. Jacobs was sent in to Fort Griffin to negotiate a sale. He made a successful deal with a man named Webb, who represented an Eastern firm. Webb was to oversee the transportation of this large quantity of hides to Fort Griffin—an undertaking of such magnitude as to require fifty wagons.

Buffalo Hunting Is Profitable

DURING ITS CAREER, the Poe-Jacobs combination was generally designated as "outside hunters" by their competitors. What placed them in that category, in the estimation of other hunters, was the fact that whenever they heard shooting in their vicinity, they forthwith gathered up their camp equipage and pushed farther out on the plains. They preferred always to be on the outer edge of the advancing line of hunters. So when they started on their final venture, they lived up to expectations, and made a long jump. This time they went to Sulphur Springs, the very farthest "outside water" known on the range.

Here they found a real hunter's paradise. On one of their prospecting trips they had ridden into that vicinity just as night was falling over the crest of the knoll. They reined their horses to a stop. Below them was the largest buffalo herd they had ever laid eyes on. The animals were milling in an excited and disturbed manner. The two Johns knew that this was sure indication of a water hole near by, which explained the presence of such a great mass of the animals.

The two men rode down in search of the water from which the herd was drinking. On and on they rode, the buffalo giving way to allow them to pass.

Four miles were covered, and yet they had not passed through the herd! Finally they discovered the source of the water supply—a spring, the waters of which flowed out over a labyrinth of deep grass, now converted into a loblolly of mud by the trampling of innumerable thousands of buffalo.

The two Johns dismounted at the head of the spring and proceeded to examine it carefully. By throwing stones at the buffalo, they were able to "shoo" them away while they satisfied their own thirst. They felt no qualms in the midst of a herd of such magnitude, for buffalo, unless enraged, were not inclined to be hostile toward human beings.

The stream ran a mile or so from the spring which brought it into being. John William and John Jay rode on until midnight before reaching a spot where they thought it safe to spread their blankets on the ground and camp for the night. A stampede of that tremendous aggregation of four-footed animals would have been certain death to any human being who might be caught in the path of the onrush of the frightened animals. Both men understood that too well to run the risk of sleeping close to such danger.

When they waked, the buffalo had already scattered themselves over the surrounding plains, although several thousand remained in the vicinity of the water. Wolves and coyotes lingered near, and were taking their turns at drinking. But they, too, were easily frightened away when stones were hurled at them.

As has already been indicated, it was always

Jacobs who was selected to make the trips to Fort Griffin as they became necessary, during the long eight months from autumn to spring, which comprised the "season." The principal reason for assigning these trips to him was that his nature demanded more "sociability" than did the temperament of John William, or even Joe McCombs. Jacobs craved the society of women more than did either of his companions. The long months on the plains without even the sight of a woman grated on him. So the others let Jacobs make the occasional trips back to Fort Griffin, and get what "society" the little town offered.

During one of Jacobs' trips the hunters' camp suffered its most serious attack by the Indians—and that during the absence of John William and Joe McCombs.

They came in one evening from the hunt, to find that the Indians had raided the camp. All the provisions were either carried away or ruined beyond use. Hundreds of hides which had been staked out to dry were slashed to pieces. Even the tepee had been burned.

But buffalo hunters were not the sort to be made despondent by destruction of their food and shelter, though they were miles from the nearest people who could help. John William told the skinner:

"Well, if we can't have bread and coffee, we can certainly have meat!"

They went back to the spot where they had killed buffalo that day and cut thick steaks from the choice hump of a fresh carcass. They made their

fire of buffalo chips where they were, and when the
meal was done—straight meat, unsalted—each
rolled in one of the green hides stripped from the
kill of the day.

John William knew the peculiarities of green
hides when the below-freezing temperature of a
plains night touched them. He watched McCombs
to see if he, also, had learned that lesson. When he
saw him roll into the hide until he looked like
nothing so much as a mummy, John William
laughed for the first time since discovery of their
ruined camp.

When morning came John Wiliam slid out of
his buffalo hide without much difficulty, though it
had frozen into a sheath. Quietly he made a fire,
then called to Joe:

"Come on, you! Let's start breakfast!"

Joe groaned and began to move. But he found
himself wound tight in that stiff cocoon of frozen
hide. John William pretended to be busy at the fire.
But if he had laughed outright, Joe's remarks—
growing louder and more profane as he wrestled
with his hide—would have drowned the sound. He
began to call to John William for help. But the
sight of his red face, working out of the slim roll of
hide was far too funny not to be enjoyed. John
William "couldn't hear." Joe yelled more loudly
still:

"Roll me over to the fire, you! Let me get
thawed out!"

John William moved over to stand and stare
and shake his head. For minutes he discussed the

problem—which he said was something absolutely new in his experience. Joe swore and rolled. John William talked of butterflies coming out of cocoons and asked Joe what he would look like when he got out of the hide.

At last he "up-ended" the prisoner. But Joe immediately toppled over on his nose and yelled furiously to be rolled, not carried. And John William, taking pity on him, stopped the horseplay and rolled Joe to the fire. But while he moved him back and forth, so that the heat of the little buffalo chip fire could thaw the side section by section, not even the thought of their disaster could keep him from laughing at Joe's appearance and his furious comments.

Even Joe could grin when he was at last thawed out. For they were frontiersmen, used to hardship as to danger. Like most of their kind, they saw the humorous side of everything. And so while they had unsalted buffalo hump for breakfast, John William described to Joe exactly how he had looked during his imprisonment in the tight-fitting hide.

Jacobs could not be expected from Fort Griffin within a week. So Joe went over to the nearest camp of buffalo hunters to try buying or borrowing enough food to serve until the supplies came in. But the negro cook of the other camp waved to empty boxes.

"Boss," he said mournfully, "we's just a stand-off for you folks. We done sent in to Griffin for grub and we sent off to the next camp and we ain't got nothing from either place."

So Joe's trip—twenty-five miles each way— produced nothing in the way of help. And when he started back, it was after dark, for the Indians were all around the hunters. Joe did not dare travel in daylight, which made the going very slow.

So for ten days John William was alone in camp, without bread, salt, or coffee. A more serious shortage was that of ammunition. John William estimated that the amount on hand would serve to beat off any attack from Indians for not longer than two days. When the Indians burned the camp, the fifty pounds of powder—generally the minimum amount in their camp arsenal—had exploded and done its part in the destruction of the camp and scattering the wreckage of cooking utensils and provisions to the four winds.

The ammunition shortage made further buffalo hunting impossible. So John William, during Joe's enforced absence, occupied his time by skinning the buffalo already killed, especially those that had been shot on the day of the Indian raid. As a final misfortune, John William, while skinning an old bull buffalo whose hide clung tenaciously to the carcass, cut himself with the sharp skinning knife, making an ugly wound in the thigh. He suffered considerable loss of blood before he could tear his shirt into strips and make a clumsy bandage. Fortunately, his excellent health and the germless air of the plains combined to bring about a quick healing of the wound, and complete recovery from the excessive loss of blood.

When six or seven days had passed, John William began to feel the extremity of his situation. He was alone and almost incapacitated, with the Indian menace always before him. And naturally he supposed that Joe's delayed return could mean but one thing—the poor fellow had fallen a victim to Indians, or to some other danger of the plains. Besides, John William was beginning to see the specter of starvation—and "buffalo straight" for a week grows tiresome.

But on the tenth day relief came. John William used to describe it in this fashion:

"It was toward night of the tenth day of Joe's absence. I had grown into the habit of staring endlessly in the direction from which I expected he would come. I remember that at this time I seemed to see what I thought were specks away out on the edge of the plains. I looked and looked, unable to focus my eyes elsewhere. They appeared to come closer, and become bigger. I began to feel hopeful, but also I was afraid that I might be mistaken. Finally the specks showed as a span of mules driven not by Joe, but by John Jay. This was better luck than I had dared to expect. Where I looked for Joe, with a few handfuls of salt and flour or meal, here was John Jay, with a new team of mules, food and ammunition! I felt that I had been saved—and truly I was."

The arrival that same night of Joe—dirty, ragged and footsore—completed the reunion. Joe told of finding the neighboring camp also short of food, and explained that he had been so long in getting back because of the slow night traveling he had done to dodge the Indians.

It was a happy camp that night. The fresh provisions were liberally drawn upon and enormous numbers of Dutch oven biscuit were baked and eaten. Joe was forgetting his days of watchfulness and nights of hard travel. He lolled beside the fire and called for more "bready"—his name for the biscuit.

"My teeth are just aching for bready," he told the others, who were as hungry for bread as the red-headed skinner.

The new mules brought by Jacobs were replacements. Before his trip to Fort Griffin, the Indians had stolen the team originally brought out by the hunters. To make his trip to "town" Jacobs had been forced to borrow a team from one of the neighboring camps. In Fort Griffin, Jacobs had bought the finest animals he could locate, and the whole Poe-Jacobs outfit was proud of the new team.

Joe McCombs christened them "Jim Grilliky" and "Sam Spattiky," names which somehow expressed his exuberant pride.

But he was gravely troubled about the mules' safety. How were they to be kept from the Indians who were daily growing more troublesome?

"Don't worry about that," John William told him. "When the Indians get that team, they'll have me along with them. And before they collect me, they'll hear this old Sharps playing a funeral anthem for them."

He patted the big buffalo gun and looked affectionately at the mules.

"Eight hundred dollars they cost us. That means just about eight hundred buffalo hides. We can't afford to lose those mules, so we won't. Let's get busy and quit worrying about Indians."

They did not ignore the possibility of another attack upon the camp. As a precaution against another explosion of powder, as well as to make storage space for the new supply of provisions, they dug a hole under the tepee and cached powder and provisions there. At John William's suggestion, they kept the new wagon close to the tepee and each evening hitched the mules to the wheels.

"I don't think any Indian is going to come right up to the door to steal the mules," he said confidently. "For I'll make my bed inside the tepee within two feet of them."

But in spite of all their precautions, the hunters waked one morning and found only a trail of small hoofprints, with moccasin tracks beside them, to remind them of eight hundred dollars' worth of mules. The trail led across one of the surrounding hills and on.

John William was too furious even to swear. But Jacobs cursed Indians in general and that red mule thief in particular.

"Now, I've got to make another long trip, clear back to Fort Griffin, for another team!" he finished.

Then, noticing John William's downcast expression, he seemed to guess that his partner was recalling his confident scheme to protect the mules.

"Cheer up! Cheer up!" he said. "We're not the only losers in this damn' wilderness. All the hunters are suffering the same way from the Injuns. I'll head for the fort right away and get us a new team. But you can bet they'll be hosses this time. Mules cost too much for this neighborhood."

Joe McCombs had done his share of Indian cursing. Now that the first shock of the loss was past, his irrepressible good humor returned—and his instinct for horseplay. He looked at the partners and said solemnly:

"There's only one way I can figure this, John William. The way them mules was tied up, right at the head of your bed, I don't see how an Injun could have stole 'em without help from inside the tepee. My notion is, John Jay was in cahoots with 'em. He wanted an excuse to go back to the fort and have another sashay with the ladies, looks to me like."

"You can buck that fool notion off right now!" Jacobs told him. "Money ain't plentiful enough, around this camp, for me to lose eight hundred round, iron cartwheels, even to see a pretty girl. That's a good high price for a buffalo hunter."

He made the trip in to Fort Griffin and returned with a pair of good horses. These did all the work required of them, if they never roused Joe and the partners to the heights of pride they had felt over the splendid mules.

The pendulum of luck swung the other way after this series of misfortunes. Shortly after their loss of the mules, the outfit made the biggest kill of the year. During the remainder of their lives, both

John William and Jacobs delighted in recalling the details.

It was on a warm morning—only a few days after Jacobs had brought out the third team of the season—that John William had the luck to make a "stand" on the buffalo. In the parlance of the hunters, a "stand" meant bringing a whole herd to the halt by killing the leading bull, then killing animal after animal that attempted to get to the front of the herd.

On this particular morning, John William had reached the windward side of the herd where the buffalo could not scent him. He had crept up to a point where he could make a "rest" by putting a crotched stick in the ground to support his heavy Sharps rifle.

A big bull led off to the right with the herd following. John William pulled the trigger and the leader fell bellowing to the ground. The smell of blood excited the others and they began to mill, bellowing and pawing the dirt. They tramped around and around in mad confusion and John William waited. Presently another big fellow took the lead, and the herd followed him toward the left. Another well-directed shot dropped the new leader.

Again and again John William checked the herd until, without having changed his position, he had killed eighty buffalo on a space of ground not more than an acre in extent. This last was quite as remarkable as the large number of buffalo killed. Buffalo hunters regarded it as evidence of superior skill to leave the carcasses in a relatively small area.

Naturally this made the skinning and handling of the hides much simpler.

It was a large performance to kill eighty buffalo in one day, and leave their carcasses scattered compactly over so small a space as an acre of ground. It would furnish a topic of conversation at Fort Griffin during the next summer, when the hunters were lounging around the stores.

Less than a week later Jacobs also got a stand. But he did not equal the score of John William. This came about as follows: A hunter was compelled to carry a canteen of water to use in cooling his rifle, which would heat excessively under the rapid fire it was subjected to. On the day of his stand, Jacobs used his water supply well before the buffalo had moved on. However, knowing that an overheated rifle would not shoot accurately, he decided to call it a day and quit, even though his score was only half of his partner's—forty killed.

John William was generally considered among his fellow hunters as an unusually good shot "on the run." In buffalo-range lingo this meant that he would pass by the animal and kill it as he went by. One day, while shooting on the run, he brought down a young cow. He passed within twenty feet of the fallen animal, following fast after the remainder of the herd. The wounded cow suddenly jumped to her feet. With lowered head and a bellow of rage, she made a mad rush at the hunter.

John William heard her bellowing close behind him. He turned just in time to put his one remaining bullet into her. It was no time for hesitation, and without pausing to note the effect of the shot, he threw aside his sixteen-pound Sharps and "legged it." Fortunately, his shot proved mortal. The cow staggered and fell uncomfortably near his heels.

The call had been close and the experience so shook John William that he went back to camp and spent the balance of the day in his blankets, trying to get himself composed. He always regarded it as one of his most narrow escapes from death.

Indians and charging buffalo were not the only dangers out on the buffalo range. Nature herself sometimes seemed to declare hostility. John William and Joe McCombs were once very near being the victims of a mirage.

On this occasion they rode their horses on a prospecting tour for new herds of buffalo. As they topped a knoll, their blood almost froze, for just a short distance in front was what appeared to be a band of Indians in full war regalia. The two men sprang from their saddles and tied their horses together, taking station behind them, ready to shoot the horses and use their bodies for breastworks, if the "Comanches" gave battle. But the "Indians" did not behave as might be expected from warriors. Instead of advancing, they merely ran back and forth.

The suspense was almost unbearable. To shoot the horses or not, was the question. Then Joe exclaimed:

"Holy Moses! They're gone!"

"But where to?" John William cried. "They've turned into a bunch of prairie dogs, that's what they've done!"

"*Damned* if they ain't!" Joe agreed.

It took the men several minutes to recover from their amazement. Then they talked for some time over the strange phenomenon that had almost trapped them into killing their horses.

"Wouldn't we have been in a pretty pickle if we had put ourselves afoot away out here on the plains, just because we were fooled by a mirage?" John William said disgustedly.

Other hardships that made life dangerous for the buffalo hunters were the torrential rains and the terrific hailstorms which came suddenly upon the plains. The Poe-Jacobs outfit suffered at least twice from heavy hailstorms.

One of these occurred in the spring, when the grass was getting tender and green. This had tempted a span of oxen belonging to the outfit to stray away a considerable distance in search of fresh grass. Jacobs and Joe McCombs went after the missing animals. All forenoon the air had been humid, and as the afternoon advanced the clouds grew darker and heavier. Suddenly Joe exclaimed:

"Holy Moses! Listen to that roar. I believe there's a hailstorm coming!"

They pulled in their horses to listen and in a few seconds the hail was beating down upon them. The stones were of such size that the men had to dismount, take the saddles off their horses and put them over their heads for protection.

"Funny sort of helmets to be wearing," Joe re-marked, with chattering teeth. "But darned if they don't seem to be saving our lives."

The horses trembled with fright and pain, and pulled at the bridle reins. The darkness that ac-companied the storm was so dense that the men were dragged by the frantic animals in opposite directions. Becoming separated, they had to make their way to camp, each as best he could. Several hours later, when they were back in camp, Jacobs turned to Joe and asked him seriously:

"What did you do during the worst of that storm?"

"Well, by heck, I tried to pray," Joe told him, just as seriously. "But all I could think of was 'Lord, give us rest!' And, by jinks, I certainly needed it! Look here!"

He displayed a head swollen and cut by the hailstones.

Another hard attack by hail occurred when the victims were John William and an employee named Thomas Kilpatrick—a "t. b." who had been hired by John William more from pity than in expecta-tion that he would become a good buffalo skinner. But the plains air had healed the young man's lungs, and his sense of obligation to his work had converted him from an awkward novice into an ex-pert who could skin fifty or more buffalo a day.

A few months after his arrival in camp, and when he was still very incompetent, he and John William were caught out in a hailstorm which took rank as one of the most severe that ever swept over the plains of western Texas. A stone of immense size struck Kilpatrick on the head with such force as to knock him instantly unconscious. Heedless of his own personal danger, John William dropped his gun and carried the injured skinner to camp on his back.

The camp had likewise suffered from the effect of the hail. The wagon sheet looked as though it had been riddled by bullets; the tin pans and other cooking utensils that had been left out around the fire were battered into shapelessness. John William carried Kilpatrick into the tepee and soon brought him back to consciousness by rubbing his hands and body and administering a strong "toddy."

At the close of the buffalo season in the spring of 1878, the Poe-Jacobs outfit drove into Fort Griffin with seventeen hundred hides, representing an equivalent number of dollars. They realized that this was probably their last hunt. The range had become overrun with hunters, who had come in increasing numbers during the six years that John William had hunted over it. The buffalo were getting scarcer and scarcer. Not only had they been killed in large numbers, but they were developing a remarkable sagacity about the situation on the plains of West Texas. They were deserting their old haunts during the winter season, and "parking" themselves farther north.

The two Johns sold all their outfit but the team. They drove over to Albany, where they hoped to find a good investment for their money. Here they stayed until some time in June, and Jacobs married. They failed to find a suitable opportunity to establish themselves, so made the long trip down to San Antonio. There, with the money received from buffalo hides, they bought fourteen hundred sheep. These they drove the hundred miles back to Albany, engaging a man to drive the wagon on the return journey; but John William and John Jay walked the entire distance, directing the bleating herd of "woolly-backs."

Jacobs' marriage necessitated some readjustment; so when the partners got back to Albany with the sheep, they discussed matters. As both were not needed to herd the sheep, they decided that the married partner was best fitted to "become stationary." Jacobs therefore elected to occupy the house on the range and look after the sheep, while John William went back to Fort Griffin to take a commission as deputy under U. S. Marshal Fleming, a position which had been offered him.

Apprentice Peace Officer

FORT GRIFFIN in the days of the trail herds and the buffalo hunters was known up and down West Texas as what the cowboys termed "an all-night hurrah town." As a newcomer and as a hunter coming in from the range, John William Poe had many times seen Griffin display its "man for breakfast."

Now, as a peace officer, the community was much more definitely his concern. He divided the population into three parts—the law-abiding element, the reckless but not really lawless men, and the toughs who understood nothing but force.

He was quickly made town marshal—the equivalent of chief of police—in addition to his commission as Deputy United States Marshal. Like Gillett of El Paso and Smith of Abilene, he policed his town without killings, and without taking a step backward from the most ferocious of those human wolves who were, just then, terrorizing all such towns as Fort Griffin.

And he found more and more to like about this new profession. When the hard winter of 1878-79 saw him—with Jacobs—a sheepman without sheep, he took his loss calmly. Both partners suffered the disaster without being cast down. Fourteen hundred sheep, representing the profits of their buffalo hunting, died from cold or lack of food. It was hard to see the price of wool skyrocketing and think of the profits they might have made.

But neither was the type to look backward. John William received a liberal salary as marshal. So they bought another herd of sheep, and once more Jacobs took charge of the "woollies." But, more and more, John William was finding the life of an officer suited to his nature.

Eventually, he sold out his interest in the sheep to Jacobs and concentrated upon his work as a peace officer.

In later years, he often remarked that a bigger greenhorn could hardly have been chosen for marshal of Fort Griffin. His first arrest he never forgot.

The man surrendered without resistance, but then—perhaps after a look at John William's pleasant face—he asked courteously if he could go over to his wagon, to get his coat. But it was not a coat he wanted. He whirled on the new marshal with a six-shooter scooped up from the wagon.

John William struck out at him instinctively and knocked the pistol out of the man's hand. Before the gun touched the ground, John William caught him and pinned his arms to his sides. He was a big man, and powerful; this man, like others in later times, found himself helpless.

Fort Griffin was a perfect "college" for a peace officer. Every sort of crime that human beings can commit was on the marshal's docket. Every type of criminal was present. The man who enforced town laws could hardly be surprised anywhere by any situation he met.

John William's service as marshal was during the activity of a vigilance committee. There were two factions in the community. One side believed sincerely that the machinery of law was not competent in the face of such widespread lawlessness as West Texas knew; and that only vigilantes could check the criminals at the time.

The other faction—and John William was one of this party—believed with equal conviction that the regular processes of law, even if imperfect, were better than the summary measures of a vigilance organization.

The two factions came to a crisis in what was known as "the Laren Case."

John Laren had come to Fort Griffin from Dodge City, Kansas. He was a man of strong and pleasant personality—a typical cowboy. He rode for a rancher named Matheson and presently married one of the boss's daughters.

His father-in-law helped him to start a brand of his own, and John Laren seemed to be on the way to success as a cowman. Everybody liked him, and he was particularly popular with the sporting element of "The Flat" in Fort Griffin.

One of his closest friends was a man named John Selman—a name of no particular importance at this time, but which was destined to become known the West over some years later, with his killing of the notorious gunman, John Wesley Hardin, in El Paso. Selman and Laren decided

that Sheriff Henry Jacobs (not to be confused with
John William's buffalo-hunting partner) could be
defeated for reëlection. So they began their campaign, and with the help of "The Flat" Laren was
elected sheriff.

For a while Laren made a sheriff who satisfied
everyone. He made John Selman chief deputy,
and law was enforced fearlessly and intelligently.
Laren's record surpassed that of all his predeces-
sors in office.

But presently men began to wonder about their
sheriff. He had a contract to supply the military
garrison of the fort with three beeves a day. And
almost immediately the ranchers of the neighborhood could meet and total their stock losses at *just*
three beeves a day.

This oddity was noticed presently. And when
it appeared that Laren's little herd remained at
about the same size, no matter how many beeves
he delivered, the cowmen began to watch. But no
evidence was found to connect the sheriff and his
deputy with rustling. However, the county's suspicions were strong enough to let Bill Cruger defeat
Laren at the following election.

As soon as Cruger was made sheriff, the cowmen demanded that he investigate the increasing
numbers of cattle lost. Even Laren's father-in-law
and brothers-in-law were among the complainants.

In the way customary on the frontier, John
William held several official posts. He was both
Deputy United States Marshal and town marshal
of Fort Griffin. Now, to give him jurisdiction in the

county, he became a deputy sheriff also. And one of the most interesting affairs to come into the sheriff's office at this time was the disappearance of a man working on the Laren ranch.

This hand of Laren's had complained to various people that he was having trouble about his wages. Laren had not paid him, and the man was doubtful about collecting what was due. When word came to Cruger's staff that the cowboy was missing, the sheriff's deputies naturally wondered if Laren had driven him off the place to avoid paying the debt— or if he had taken even grimmer measures, and more effective, to stop the cowboy's protests.

There was also the possibility that this man had known too much about the mysterious Laren way of furnishing beef to the fort without diminishing the size of his herd.

A "tip" came to Cruger as the sheriff began a quiet investigation. A "nester," as the cow country termed a small farmer or rancher, suggested that the sheriff drag a deep hole in the Clear Fork near town.

"Just to see what you find," this man, Lancaster by name, said cautiously.

John William was among the deputies who acted upon this hint. And some two hundred cowhides were brought up from the water. Almost every brand and earmark known in the vicinity was represented among those telltale hides.

While Cruger studied this evidence, Mrs. Lancaster came into town. She was badly frightened. Lancaster had ridden out and failed to come home.

Cruger knew that if Laren and Selman had guessed the name of his informant, Lancaster's life would be forfeit. He sent a deputy, Jim Draper, to hunt for the nester. Draper's posse found Lancaster the next day, seriously wounded, hiding in the brakes along the river.

"Who shot you?" Draper demanded of Lancaster.

The nester was slow to tell; he had been frightened and he was afraid, now, that death would come to him if he testified against Laren. But he was persuaded to admit that Laren and Selman had come looking for him and had chased him for miles the day before, shooting at him.

"I barely got away," he said. "And I was afraid to go home, then. I thought they might follow me up to the house and kill my whole family."

Draper assured him that Laren and Selman would soon be powerless to harm him.

"You're going over to the county seat right now," he told Lancaster. "You're going to swear out a warrant for Laren and Selman, for trying to kill you."

And the posse escorted Lancaster to Albany to bolster up his courage. Then Draper went triumphantly back to the sheriff, carrying warrants for the two bushwhackers.

Cruger knew that Laren and Selman had many friends among the lawless element of the county. It was understood that at least twenty desperadoes would follow them at a call. So he moved cautiously to make his arrests. His posse was large enough to face any support that Laren could raise, and he led it out of town after dark, to "keep the news behind him."

The posse reached the Laren ranch before daylight and hid near the corral. Laren was a dead shot, and his attempt to murder Lancaster proved him desperate. Cruger wondered how he could make the arrest without having his own men killed. But Laren made matters easy for the officers.

Daylight came while the posse sprawled behind such cover as the ranch yard offered. Laren came out with a milk pail on his arm, moving toward the corral, and toward the waiting men.

"Look!" John William whispered to Cruger. "He didn't put his six-shooter on!"

And he and Cruger watched tensely while the unsuspecting Laren walked straight toward them. When he was covered by a dozen rifles and pistols, Cruger and John William jumped from behind their shelter and leveled pistols at the ex-sheriff.

"Put 'em up, Laren," Cruger called. "I've got a warrant for you."

Laren looked from face to face of the posse and shook his head.

"Well, if that's not nearly hell," he said disgustedly. "It's the first time in my life *I* was ever caught without a gun on—or a chance to grab one. I suppose you feel pretty good. Well, I'll hand you five hundred dollars if you'll let my wife bring my pistol out. Then I'll take my chances with you and your whole damned outfit!"

"I didn't come out here to listen to you," Cruger

told him flatly. "I came out to serve a warrant and I'm serving it."

"No, you're too big a coward to stand up to me, without everything in your favor. You wouldn't face me if I had a gun."

"Never mind the blowing," Cruger said quietly. "It won't do you a bit of good here. I'm not taking an unnecessary chance with these men's lives, just to let you play hero."

He turned to John William and two other deputies.

"Handcuff the scoundrel!" he ordered them shortly.

When Laren was handcuffed and mounted on a horse, the posse tied his feet together beneath the animal's belly. The trip to Albany was made by way of Fort Griffin. Word of the capture had gone ahead, and Laren's friends in "The Flat" gathered for a demonstration. But the grim faces and ready guns of the posse checked the desperadoes, and Cruger took his prisoner on toward the county seat.

Albany had no jail at the time, so Laren was held in a private house under guard. Cruger had been made uneasy by the incident in Fort Griffin. He expected the Laren faction to make some attempt at rescue. So he chose guards from among the most reliable men of his deputies and the posse. John William was one of the first chosen.

The sheriff's uneasiness was justified. John Selman began to recruit as soon as news of Laren's arrest came to him. He gathered a large number of gunmen for a descent on Albany.

There was still a third element involved—the Fort Griffin Vigilance Committee. This group met when word of Selman's recruiting came to town. It was decided by the vigilantes that Laren had run his course. If Selman were permitted to rescue the rustling, murdering ex-sheriff, the county could expect little less than civil war before Laren and his men were arrested or killed or driven off by the law-abiding citizens.

The committee acted quickly. They armed and mounted themselves and set out for Albany in a race with Selman's thugs. As they rode fast for the county seat they listened for sound of the rescuers.

In Albany, John William was captain of the guards watching Laren for the first half of the night. At eleven-thirty he looked at his watch and told his men that they had only a half-hour to go.

"Then the other bunch can have this job," he said, "and welcome to it!"

He stepped out of the house which they were using for a jail—and the vigilantes swarmed around him. The night was misty, and they had slipped up soundlessly to surround the place. They held John William helpless and disarmed him while some twenty of the committee rushed into the house and covered the remaining guard with their rifles.

Laren had been sleeping on a bench. He sat up to face the vigilantes and, whatever his faults were, Laren was a brave man. He asked the leader what he wanted.

"You!" the vigilantes' chief said grimly. "The

time has come when you pass in your checks. You've been leading a double life too long. You played up to the decent people in the county, and all the time you were hand-in-hand with the gang that's been doing all the dirty work in this part of the country. Hundreds of beef steers have been stolen around here, and their hides have been found in the Clear Fork close to your place. And there's plenty of suspicion that you murdered more than one of your hands that disappeared. Have you got anything to say?"

"I haven't got a thing in God's world to say to you or any of your cowardly gang," Laren answered. "You sneaked up here and captured the sheriff's guards after he promised me a fair trial. All I've got to say is this: Take the cuffs off me and put a gun in my hand, and I'll take on your whole outfit. And I'll promise you that gang of yours will need a new boss in two seconds. But I know there's no use talking to you. Go ahead—I'll take anything you can hand out, straight!"

"All right," the vigilante chief told him. "We're not going to hang you. You did some good when you were sheriff, so we'll use our shooting irons on you."

He turned to the men behind him and jerked his head:

"All right, boys! Step up and do your duty."

Eleven men filed up and quietly lifted their Winchesters. Laren threw back his shoulders.

"Come on," he yelled at them. "Do your dirty work—shoot me to hell as quick as you can!"

As the volley roared in the house John Selman and his "rescuers" had reached the west side of town. They pulled in their horses when the shots sounded from the "jail."

"No use, boys," Selman told his gang. "The stranglers beat us to him. It's our necks we've got to think about now. Let's get out of this!"

And the Laren Gang whirled around and raced into the misty darkness. John Selman by various roads came to El Paso and became a notable of sorts in that frontier community, until he died some fifteen-odd years later under the gunfire of Deputy United States Marshal Scarborough.

This Laren case was not the most interesting of John William's experience in his time at Fort Griffin, although it was an episode about which he always felt strongly. Each day of service as deputy sheriff or town marshal or United States Marshal brought its work and its dangers. Fugitive killers from other regions were located and arrested; cowboys "on the prod" had to be quieted or arrested; fights and murders rose in gambling hells and dance places; mysterious disappearances were reported and must be investigated.

It was a full and busy life. One complicated case, which dragged on beyond the end of John William's term of service in Fort Griffin, was the Lassiter affair—here treated as an appendix.

John William was becoming restless in town. He heard of new regions being settled and the open country drew him. So, in the fall of 1879 he "pulled up stakes" once more.

Trailing "Billy the Kid"

☆

THE PANHANDLE of Texas was being settled in 1879, and opportunities to make money rapidly presented themselves to the pioneer. John William moved from Fort Griffin to Wheeler County and settled in Fort Elliott near Mobeetie, Wheeler's county seat.

He continued to serve as a peace officer, and his record as Deputy United States Marshal and deputy sheriff was so impressive that he was persuaded to campaign for the office of sheriff.

The lawless element of the county was solidly against him. When election day came, the opposition's vote was marshaled and sent down to the polls. John William's supporters were overconfident. J. S. McCarthy, manager of the Littlefield Cattle Company (the famous LFD brand) was typical. He gathered fifteen LFD cowboys for the trip to town, then said:

"Ah, there's no use of it. It's a long trip, and Poe can't fail to be elected. We'll stay home."

Others felt the same way, and the Poe ticket was defeated by one vote. Then John William's supporters collected five hundred dollars and came to him to offer the amount as a fund with which to contest the election. But John William was irritated and he refused.

"You slept on your rights," he told the committee, "and I'm not going to carry the matter any farther."

Presently, he was not sorry that he had failed to become Wheeler County's sheriff. A larger opportunity offered itself.

Canadian River cattlemen had suffered serious losses from stock thieves, and to stamp out rustling they organized a Cattlemen's Association. A competent stock detective was needed, and without hesitation the Association turned to John William Poe. He accepted the position and began to ride the range, identifying the thieves, becoming acquainted with their methods and connections and making arrests.

It was a difficult assignment in that wild region. Sometimes the county officers were not sympathetic to an outsider who came in asking their assistance—as when John William went to Trinidad, Colorado, to bring back a Mexican wanted in Texas for rustling. He was a Deputy United States Marshal, and his extradition papers were in order. But when he appeared at the railway station with his prisoner, the local sheriff—a Mexican—interfered.

Not only did he free the Mexican rustler and send him out of town, but he arrested John William and without ceremony threw him into jail. John William submitted quietly, but sent a telegram to the United States Marshal, his superior.

The sheriff was jerked up by a telegram from the Marshal, ordering him to free his subordinate and restore the prisoner, or suffer the consequences. The result was a complete apology and promise to have the Mexican rustler at the station the next morning—a promise kept to the letter.

William H. Bonney, known far and wide over the Western country as "Billy the Kid," was already notorious as a cow rustler and horse thief when John William began his detective work along the Canadian River.

Oddly, this hazel-eyed youngster who was to lead a gang of Western desperadoes came out of New York slums, born there November 23, 1859. But virtually all of his life was spent on the frontier, for his mother operated eating houses in one "camp" after another.

This is not the place to tell Billy's story. John William Poe was concerned with young Bonney as a stock thief, not as the desperado who terrorized Lincoln County and much of New Mexico. And so it is enough to say that after a career which carried him over the Southwest, Billy—"The Kid"— drifted into southwestern New Mexico and worked for a young Englishman named John Tunstall. But Tunstall was brutally murdered at the beginning of the Lincoln County War of 1878 and 1879, and the Kid, swearing revenge upon those connected with the killing of his friend, became involved in shooting affrays that brought on several killings, most of which were laid to him.

After the Lincoln County War had subsided, the Kid became the leader of an organized band of desperadoes, although himself under the age of

twenty-one. He was a born leader, and the gang
began to terrorize eastern New Mexico and adjacent
sections of Texas. Cattle and horses were stolen;
murder was committed whenever an owner interfered with the operations of the Kid's gang. At last,
however, the law-abiding people became awakened
to the necessity of ridding the country of this undesirable element. John William, as representative
of the Canadian Cattlemen's organization, found it
to be his duty to try to eliminate the Kid's gang.

Soon after he entered upon this task, John William went to New Mexico to learn at first hand who
purchased the cattle stolen by the Kid's gang in the
Panhandle and always driven into New Mexico.
Though John William was interested in this particular point, he also had a hope that he might bring
about the capture of the Kid himself.

He rode all the way on horseback to White
Oaks, a newly developed mining town in Lincoln
County. In his pocket he carried a letter from
Charles Goodnight, a millionaire stockman of
Texas, and one of the leading spirits of the Cattle-
men's Association. Through the men to whom this
letter was addressed, John William was able to
gain much information that led him to investigate
about the ranch of one Pat Coghlin, on the Tres
Rios (Three Rivers).

The game proved to be well worth the candle,
for he actually found fourteen hides drying on the
fence, and every hide bore the brands of the Canadian Cattle Company.

Before Coghlin had become aware of an officer's presence on his place, John William had him under arrest. Like the coward he was, Coghlin begged for mercy. He offered John William large sums to be liberated; but John William was always inflexible when it came to a question of right and wrong. So it came about that in the course of time, Coghlin was indicted by the grand jury at Mesilla.

When John William was waiting for court to convene, he occupied himself trying to locate others who were associated with the Kid's activities in the Canadian Cattle Company's stock. Just about that time, December, 1880, Sheriff Pat Garrett and a fighting posse captured the Kid at Arroyo Tivan, surrounding him and four companions in a deserted rock house.

At the March term of court in 1881, the Kid was tried at Mesilla. He was convicted of the murder of Sheriff Brady in Lincoln, during April, 1878. The young desperado was sent to Lincoln in custody of Sheriff Garrett to await the date of his execution, which was to be in May, 1881.

Some time in April, Garrett came to White Oaks on official business, and learning of John William's presence there, hunted him up. They discussed matters of common interest as officers of the law. As a result of this meeting, John William decided to go down to Tombstone, Arizona. It was supposed other members of the Kid's gang were rustling cattle in that neighborhood, for their operations now reached from the Texas Panhandle through New Mexico and into Arizona.

This trip occupied a few weeks, after which John William returned to White Oaks. He had been in town but a few days when word came from Lincoln that on April 28 Billy the Kid had killed his two guards and escaped from jail—just two days before the date set for his hanging! That bit of news was the sensation of the whole Southwest! Those who sympathized with the Kid—and they were many—rejoiced; but the cattlemen swore furiously at the word.

On the day of the Kid's sensational escape Garrett was in White Oaks, and he started immediately for Lincoln. But before leaving, he arranged with John William for the latter to remain in White Oaks and keep a vigilant outlook for the Kid, as none could surmise in which direction this young daredevil would choose to go, or where he would look for refuge. It was not improbable that he would remain close to the scene of his narrow escape from the hangman's noose; in fact, it would be quite in keeping with his inclination to do what would be theatrical.

Garrett was prompt in organizing posses and sending them out in every direction, with instructions to take no chances, but to bring in the young desperado dead or alive. However, after several weeks of fruitless search, he was almost ready to give up the hunt. He was more and more convinced that the Kid had made his way down into Old Mexico.

All this time, John William had remained in White Oaks, quietly ferreting out those cattle rustlers who were still committing depredations in that neighborhood. He was constantly on the look-out for stolen cattle, and now and then found hides bearing the brand of his company. Whenever it was possible for Garrett to leave his own duties—which were particularly arduous at that time—he would come over to White Oaks and assist John William in making arrests and tracking down desperate characters, who were numerous enough in that vicinity.

Early one morning during July of 1881, John William was roused by a light knocking on the door of his hotel room. He got out of bed quickly and went to the door, pistol in hand:

"Who's there?" he demanded.

"Let me in—quick! And for God's sake, don't make a noise!" a man whispered.

John William opened the door cautiously, and a dark figure almost jumped into the unlighted room.

"I don't want anybody to know about my coming to you. I've got something important to tell you. It's about the Kid."

John William put down his gun and began to get into his clothes. He could scarcely see the man's face in the faint light of early dawn. He asked him who he was.

"I'm Quinn—remember me? You helped me out, over in Texas. You kept me from going wrong, and I never forgot it. So I want to help you. I know what you're after, over here, and I happened onto some important information. Is it safe to talk?"

He looked suspiciously around the room, as he had done upon entering it.

"It's safe enough," John William reassured him. "Safe to talk here and safe to tell me anything you want to. What is it?"

He recalled the man, now. Quinn was a heavy drinker and seemed unable to break the habit. But he was no liar and he would stand by anyone he considered his friend.

"I know where the Kid is!" Quinn said shakily. "I've been sleeping here and there, wherever I could. A few nights ago I turned in on the hay in a livery stable. The two partners running the place are friends of the Kid. Well, I was waked by them talking, and when I heard *his* name mentioned I listened close. Mr. Poe—the Kid's not in Mexico! He never has been in Mexico. He's over at Fort Sumner hiding in his *querida's* house. And he's been right here in White Oaks since he broke out. That's what those fellows said."

"It's not possible!" John William told him incredulously. "He wouldn't be foolish enough to show himself here, where everybody knows him; not after murdering Bell and Ollinger."

But the more he considered it, the less incredible Quinn's story seemed. After all, where would the Kid find more friends to shelter him than in his old haunts? He must know that Garrett believed him in Mexico. So Fort Sumner, even White Oaks, would be the logical place to lie low.

"Well, I can't swear to it," Quinn admitted. "But it sounded straight to me, and I thought you'd want to know. All I'm asking is that you don't let my name slip into it anywhere. There are plenty of his friends around who'd put a slug in me if they had the ghost of an idea I'd talked."

John William promised to keep the source of the information a secret, and Quinn slipped out of the room.

He thought about the matter from all angles and was not long in making up his mind that it deserved investigation. So he went to Lincoln and told Sheriff Pat Garrett.

"Nonsense!" Garrett exploded, when he heard the story. "The Kid's in Old Mexico by this time. He wouldn't take a chance on hanging around where everybody knows him; not with a price on his head."

John William argued that the Kid would find it hard to leave his lady friends behind; and that with most of the Mexicans either afraid of him, or actually his friends, he might feel safer close to his old haunts than in a strange place.

"All right," Garrett gave in at last. "We'll go to Roswell and pick up Kip McKinney and give your idea a chance."

In Roswell, Deputy Sheriff McKinney shook his head as Garrett had done:

"Not a chance of the Kid's being in Sumner," he said. "But if Pat wants to make the trip, it's all right with me."

When the three of them rode out of town it was separately, and none headed toward Fort Sumner. Even Garrett agreed that if the Kid really had

lingered in this neighborhood, there would be
friends quick to carry news of officers riding toward his supposed hiding place.

When out of sight of those who might be watching, they rejoined each other and went straight toward their objective. They slept on their saddle
blankets near the picketed horses that night, and on
the next day rode fifty miles. Late in the afternoon
a halt was made among some sand hills to hold
council.

"The bunch of us can't ride into Sumner and
hope to pass without being noticed," Garrett said.
"Poe is a stranger there. If he goes in, he can inquire around and maybe find out if the Kid really
is around the place."

John William agreed to this.

"Beaver Smith's store is the place to go first,"
Garrett instructed him. "But if you don't get anything in town, go on out to Rudolph's ranch. The
place is called Sunnyside; it's about seven miles
north of town. I'll give you a note saying you're a
friend of mine, and Rudolph will take care of you.
I think you can trust him. If the Kid's around,
Rudolph ought to know it."

When they had set upon a place to meet after
John William's scout to Sumner, he rode on into the
settlement. Fort Sumner, this July day of 1881,
was an abandoned military post. The population
was perhaps three hundred, all but a dozen or two
being Mexicans. Of the Americans, few but were
of undesirable character, and naturally the sort to
be in sympathy with the Kid.

At Beaver Smith's, John William was closely studied by everyone in and about the store-saloon. Men asked him where he was going, and why; who he was; where he had been—all the questions a hostile community could think of. He gave them as plausible a yarn as possible, saying he was a prospector from White Oaks, going back to his old home in the Panhandle.

He bought drinks, and so did some of the others. But he was careful to swallow only a small part of his liquor. When suspicion of him seemed to have died down, he said something about Billy the Kid—and instantly everyone stared at him. He bought another round of drinks and dropped the subject. Presently he went out to a restaurant and ate. When he had finished his meal he loitered around the village for two or three hours, talking casually to everyone he met.

The reaction he got each time to his remarks and questions made him sure that Fort Sumner knew something about the Kid. The atmosphere was very tense, and he had the feeling that all these people were expecting something to happen.

As he wandered around, he was surprised to meet a very familiar figure crossing the street. It was John Jacobs, and the two former partners stared amazedly at each other. But John William controlled himself quickly. Before Jacobs could call his name, he made their old danger signal, and Jacobs came up to him with a blank face.

"Where's your camp?" John William whispered and when he had received the location in the same guarded tone, he said: "See you there, sometime after dark. Go on, now."

He had decided to go out to Rudolph's and try pumping the rancher about the Kid.

He got his horse and covered the seven miles to Sunnyside. Rudolph was home and after he had read Pat Garrett's letter of introduction he was quite cordial. He asked John William to stop the night, took charge of his horse, and escorted him in to supper.

But as soon as John William mentioned the Kid —he said he had heard that the little outlaw was hiding around Fort Sumner—Rudolph became very nervous.

"I have heard that story," he said quickly. "But I cannot believe it. The Kid is far too shrewd to stay here, when the officers are hunting him and there is a price on his head."

John William studied his host. He decided that Rudolph was a man of good intentions but, like many others in New Mexico, was in mortal terror of the little desperado.

"Look here, Mr. Rudolph," he said abruptly. "I came to Fort Sumner to look for the Kid. Pat Garrett sent me to you, because he feels that if the Kid really is around Sumner, you know about it and you ought to be willing to help us capture him. You can trust me. Now, what do you know about the Kid?"

"Nothing!" Rudolph insisted. "Absolutely nothing. If he is in Fort Sumner, I don't know it.

And I can't believe that he would come to a place where he's so well known. He——"

And he repeated everything he had said at first. John William, listening, felt more certain than at first that Quinn's story had been correct; that the Kid really was somewhere in this vicinity; and that Rudolph knew it.

"Almost dark," he said in a careless tone. "My horse is rested, and we've both eaten. I think I'll change my mind and ride on, Mr. Rudolph."

"You know you are perfectly welcome to stay the night," Rudolph said, but there was relief in his expression.

He continued to assure John William that he was "more than welcome" to stay overnight while he saw his guest saddling. And when John William met Garrett and Kip McKinney on the far side of Fort Sumner, Rudolph's manner still rode with him.

"Pat," he told the lanky sheriff of Lincoln County, "that little devil is around here, just as Quinn said he is. They all know it and even if they'd really like to see him caught, they're afraid to say anything."

"I still think it's a wild-goose chase," Garrett answered skeptically. "The Kid's in Old Mexico."

"I can't believe it—not after watching Rudolph," John William persisted. "But let's take a little ride over to see a friend of mine. He's camped beyond town and he'll give us supper. We can talk it over at Jacobs' camp."

Jacobs had come to Fort Sumner to buy sheep,

and his camp was separated from the town only by high dunes. The three sat down by his fire, and Jacobs cooked supper for the visitors. He had heard a great deal of John William's reputation as an officer, and the two old friends had a great deal to talk out. But after a time of reminiscing, John William turned to Pat Garrett and once more went over the ground, giving his reasons for believing that Billy the Kid was in Fort Sumner or had been there recently. At last Garrett said:

"All right, you win. I still think it's a cold trail, but I know a house where one of his girls lives. If the Kid's in Sumner, or anywhere around, we ought to find him going in or coming out there. We'll take a look at the house. We can leave the horses in a motte of trees close to town, then hide in a peach orchard behind the girl's place."

John William explained to Jacobs enough of their errand to let his old partner understand that it was dangerous business they were on. They shook hands, and John William, Garrett, and McKinney mounted.

They rode through the brilliant moonlight to the grove of trees Garrett had mentioned. There they hitched the horses and went on to the peach orchard. Here they watched the girl's house from nine o'clock until after eleven.

"I told you it's a cold trail!" Garrett said finally, in disgust. "If the Kid was here we'd have seen him coming or going from that house. Let's get out of here before the town knows we came in hunting the Kid."

John William was still playing his hunch. But Garrett's stand did seem like common sense.

"There must be somebody besides Rudolph to ask," he told Garrett. "How about this fellow Maxwell? He's a big sheepman; he's got a stake in the country; he ought to be glad to see outlaws like the Kid caught. Let's ask him what he knows or has heard."

"All right," Garrett agreed. "He lives in the old officers' quarters on the parade ground. I know the way."

He led them by roundabout paths to the long, one-story 'dobe building which sat behind a paling fence end-to the street, where Pedro Maxwell lived. The three went into the yard, and on the porch Garrett said:

"That's Maxwell's room in the corner. You fellows wait here while I go in and talk to him."

John William sat down on the porch near a gate at its end. McKinney squatted on his heels in the grass alongside, both men being rather in the shadows. They talked in guarded whispers. Garrett had disappeared through an open door only a few feet from where the two deputies silently awaited the outcome of his interview with Maxwell.

About thirty seconds after Garrett had entered Maxwell's room, John William noticed a man walking along the inside of the picket fence which fronted the building. He was about fifty feet away and seemed to be in his stocking feet. John William watched him, but with no particular care.

"Some friend of Maxwell's—or maybe Maxwell himself," he thought.

McKinney made no comment—possibly had not observed the soft-footed stranger approaching.

The man arrived within arm's length of John William before he saw the two men in the shadows. Like a flash he sprang upon the veranda, whipping out his six-shooter and covering both men. At the same time he demanded in Spanish:

"*Quien es? Quien es?* Who is it?" As the man repeated the question rapidly, he backed toward the door through which Garrett had just entered.

"Oh, you needn't be afraid," John William said reassuringly as he rose and moved toward the stranger. "We're not going to hurt you."

By some strange whim of Fate, both John William and Kip McKinney escaped death in that fraction of time. Neither guessed that it might be Billy the Kid.

But something kept the man's finger from pulling the trigger of his weapon. Instead, he backed into the open doorway of Maxwell's room, where he paused for just an instant, with his body concealed by the thick 'dobe wall at the side of the door. His head came out—and his pistol.

"*Quien es?*" he called again.

Then he disappeared through the doorway.

From his position, John William could not see what happened during the next few seconds within that darkened room, but he distinctly overheard every word.

"Pete," a sharp voice exclaimed, "who are those two fellows out there on the porch?"

There was silence for a second. Then came the explosion of a pistol, instantly followed by another shot. John William jumped to a position in front of the door, but, because of the darkness of the room, could see nothing. He heard a groan, then two or three gasps, "like someone dying." Suddenly Pat Garrett rushed out of the room, brushing against John William. His gun was in his hand.

"I killed the Kid!" he blurted. "I killed the Kid!"

"Killed the Kid?" both deputies repeated.

Then John William exclaimed:

"Pat, you *must* have killed the wrong man. The Kid would never come here. Not to Maxwell's."

"I wonder if I did?" Garrett said doubtfully. Then:

"No, I killed the Kid. I know his voice too well to be mistaken."

At that instant Pete Maxwell came dashing from the room. John William at once "threw down" on the man with his Colt. He would have shot him down instantly had not Garrett knocked the gun aside.

"Don't shoot—that's Maxwell!" he exclaimed.

In after years John William often remarked that he was glad his hand was stayed; but at the moment he supposed they were in a place infested with enemies and he proposed to take no chances. He later learned that Maxwell was not in league with the Kid. He was a well-meaning man, but rather weak in character; and with the Kid terrorizing the community, he was afraid to refuse him shelter. The result was that the Kid, thinking Maxwell's place would be above suspicion, stayed there on many occasions.

There was no further sound in the room where the shooting had occurred, so Garrett and the others felt that they might safely enter. Pete Maxwell brought a candle and placed it on the outside sill of the window. By this dim light they saw a man lying at full length on the floor. His right hand still clutched a six-shooter; in his left was a long butcher knife.

"Well, that's the Kid," Garrett announced. "He won't bother this section any longer."

Turning the body over, they found that Garrett's first shot had penetrated the breast just above the heart. The second shot had gone wild. Doubtless the Kid never knew what hit him.

Garrett then recounted to John William and McKinney just what had occurred while he was in the room. He had placed his Winchester against the wall beside the outer door and walked over to the bed in a corner of the room, to wake Maxwell. Sitting upon the edge of the bed, well up toward the head, he had just begun to question the sheepman when he heard voices on the veranda, which put him on his guard.

He stopped talking and listened.

Suddenly a man burst into the room, and, running across to the bed, inquired excitedly of Maxwell:

"Pete, who are those fellows out there on the porch?"

"I recognized the Kid's voice," Garrett said, "and I knew that just as soon as his eyes got used to the darkness of the room he would see me there. It was a question of getting there first without missing. Luckily, I hadn't taken off my six-shooter. But while I was trying to work my hand down where I could make a quick draw, the Kid noticed me, though I don't think he knew who it was. Anyway, he turned his gun on me like a flash, then began backing off. Then he demanded of me in Spanish:

" '*Quien es? Quien es?*'

"I didn't dare answer. He would have recognized my voice at once, for the Kid and I were too well acquainted to mistake one another. I didn't even try to get up from the edge of the bed, but made a 'hip shot.' Why the Kid didn't fire at me without speaking, I can't understand. Maybe he thought I was one of Maxwell's friends, and he didn't want to make a killing without knowing who it was. Anyhow, he was just too late. I got there first, and he dropped."

By this time the noise of the shooting had roused the natives, and they began to crowd around Maxwell's place. When they learned that the Kid was dead, they began bewailing the death of their *amigo* as they called the Kid. Several of the women begged to be allowed to take charge of the body.

Garrett gave his permission, and Billy the Kid's body was carried into an old carpenter shop near by and carefully laid out on a bench. Lighted candles

were set about it, in the Mexican parallel of a
"wake."

As the body was carried out of Maxwell's, John
Jacobs came running up, out of breath, carrying
his gun. He saw John William and relaxed.

"I was just falling asleep when I heard the
shots," he panted. "I was afraid I wouldn't see you
alive, but I grabbed up my gun and came running."

It was typical, not merely of John Jacobs, but of
frontier friendship. The little matter of finding
himself in a fight with all of Fort Sumner had not
checked Jacobs for an instant; not when a friend
of his might be in danger.

This was July 14, 1881, just before midnight.
Garrett and the others spent the rest of the night
in Maxwell's house. They could hear the friends
of "Billito" down at the carpenter shop and they
rather expected some sort of hostilities from friends
of the outlaw. So they sat up with guns ready. But
no move was made against them, and in the morning the *alcalde* was called.

When a coroner's jury was empaneled, none
other than the timid Mr. Rudolph was foreman of
the body. A verdict of justifiable homicide was
brought in, with a sort of postscript, in which the
community's thanks were offered to Sheriff Garrett for removing the young desperado.

Later in the day—July 15—the Kid was buried
beside Charley Bowdre and Bigfoot Tom O'Fol-
liard, good friends of his, in the old military cemetery of Fort Sumner. The curtain was down on the
grinning outlaw who, though but twenty-one years

old, had probably killed more men than any other gunman of New Mexico.

And John William went back to his work. Billy the Kid was only one thief, if an important one, in a country full of thieves. Particularly, there was the case of Pat Coghlin, sometimes called "King of the Tularosa." Coghlin had been indicted in the matter of those fourteen Canadian cowhides John William had found on his ranch.

John William knew very well that Coghlin was the sort of man who would knife his best friend for a price, but the case against him was airtight. A couple named Nesbit, man and wife, honest Scotch folks, had been subpoenaed as witnesses against Coghlin. As employes of "the King" they knew of his purchase of stolen cattle from Billy the Kid's gang, and his trick of butchering the animals and selling the meat to the quartermaster at Fort Stanton.

John William went to Mesilla for the trial. But the prosecution's witnesses failed to appear. Inquiry proved that they had started from the Coghlin ranch to attend court, taking with them their ten-year-old daughter. Search of the road disclosed the Nesbits' bodies near the famous White Sands of New Mexico.

The Nesbits had talked with neighbors before starting out. Mrs. Nesbit had been afraid. She told some of her friends:

"I'm afraid to cross the White Sands. So many terrible things have happened there."

When discovered, the bodies were only partly

clothed. Nesbit's coat and his wife's shawl were missing. The murderers had ridden away on their horses. The natural belief in New Mexico was that Coghlin's hired assassins had done the work, as the evidence of the Nesbits would certainly have sent him to the penitentiary.

The murder of these good people was a dastardly crime, and everyone hoped that the criminals would be brought to justice. Secret Service men were put on the trail, but four years passed before the killers were located across the border in Old Mexico. Two Mexicans were identified by their possession of Nesbit's coat and his wife's shawl.

One of the men turned state's evidence. He admitted that Coghlin had hired him and the other man to kill the Nesbits at the White Sands. He said his partner had killed the two adults and had then ordered him to shoot the little girl. She was begging for her life, and he had refused to commit the murder until his accomplice threatened to kill him if he refused.

Four years is a long time, and the Mexicans could not identify Coghlin when he and nineteen other men were brought into court. So "the King of the Tularosa" went free. One of the Mexicans was hanged; the state's witness was given life imprisonment. But from that time, Coghlin's star declined. He lost his wealth. His wife died, and when he followed her he was a poor and lonely old man. His ranch later became part of the noted Three Rivers Ranch, owned by Albert B. Fall, later taken over by the Doheny interests.

Buffalo herd of the skinning days. Courtesy of the Western History Collections, University of Oklahoma Library.

Forty thousand buffalo hides ready for shipment at Dodge City, Kansas, 1877. Courtesy of the Western History Collections, University of Oklahoma Library.

Dodge City, Kansas, 1878. Courtesy of the Western History Collections, University of Oklahoma Library.

John Selman after leaving Fort Griffin. Courtesy of the Western History Collections, University of Oklahoma Library.

John Wesley Hardin as a young man.
Courtesy of the Western History
Collections, University of Oklahoma
Library.

Billy the Kid. Courtesy of the Western
History Collections, University of
Oklahoma Library.

NOTICE!
TO THIEVES, THUGS, FAKIRS AND BUNKO-STEERERS,
Among Whom Are

J. J. HARLIN, alias "OFF WHEELER;" SAW DUST CHARLIE, WM. HEDGES, BILLY THE KID, Billy Mullin, Little Jack, The Cuter, Pock-Marked Kid, and about Twenty Others:

If Found within the Limits of this City after TEN O'CLOCK P. M., this Night, you will be Invited to attend a GRAND NECK-TIE PARTY,

The Expense of which will be borne by

100 Substantial Citizens.

Las Vegas, March 24th, 1881.

Notice of warning to Billy the Kid and other outlaws. Courtesy of the Western History Collections, University of Oklahoma Library.

Three famous Lincoln County sheriffs. Left to right: Pat Garrett, Jim Brent, and John William Poe. Courtesy of the Western History Collections, University of Oklahoma Library.

Catherine McCarty Antrim, Billy the Kid's
mother. Courtesy of the Western History
Collections, University of Oklahoma Library.

Pete Maxwell and Henry Leis. Courtesy of the Western History Collections, University of Oklahoma Library.

Pete Maxwell's old house at Fort Sumner. Courtesy of the Western History Collections, University of Oklahoma Library.

Captain J. C. Lea's house in Roswell, 1883. Courtesy of Special Collections, University of Arizona Library.

Captain J. C. Lea and John William Poe at a cattlemen's convention
about 1889. Courtesy of Special Collections, University of Arizona
Library.

John S. Chisum, the most prominent New Mexico cowman of the
1870s and 1880s. Courtesy of the Western History Collections, University of Oklahoma Library.

John Chisum's "splendid new" ranch house near Roswell, 1885.
Courtesy of the Western History Collections, University of Oklahoma
Library.

Lincoln, N.M., at the time of the Lincoln County War. Courtesy of the Western History Collections, University of Oklahoma Library.

From left to right: James Dolan, Emil Fritz, William Martin[?], and Major Murphy. Courtesy of the Western History Collections, University of Oklahoma Library.

The old county jail and courthouse at Lincoln, N.M. Courtesy of the Western History Collections, University of Oklahoma Library.

The old Murphy, Riley & Dolan Store opposite the Lincoln County courthouse. (The sign shows Dolan's name only because he had bought his partners out before the photograph was taken.) Courtesy of the Western History Collections, University of Oklahoma Library.

The torreon.

Ruins of the torreon at Lincoln, N.M. New Mexico State Planning
Office Collection, Richard Federici, photographer.

Officers at Fort Stanton, N.M., 1883. (Lieutenant Pershing is marked
with an X.)

Major Llewellyn, agent at Mescalero, in his militia uniform. Courtesy of C. L. Sonnichsen.

The store established by John William Poe in Roswell.

Col. A. J. Fountain, murdered near White Sands, N.M. Courtesy of the Museum of New Mexico.

John William Poe in 1924. Photo by Rodden. Courtesy of the Museum of New Mexico.

A "Gal Tenderfoot" Arrives.

ENTERS NOW the woman in the case. . . .

At this point I must shift the emphasis for a few chapters from my husband to myself, and trace my own early life in order to show how I likewise came to New Mexico and, from 1881 to this date, have made it my abiding place.

The early part of my girlhood was spent under the happiest of conditions, first in California and later at Leon, Nicaragua. But the death of my father, Fred Henry Alberding, while we resided in Nicaragua, wrought a great change in our circumstances.

My mother, after a futile attempt to develop the Nicaraguan plantation Father had started, brought us back to California. She, too, passed away in 1872, so we five children were left alone in straitened circumstances.

Mary, my eldest sister, was a beautiful girl of nearly fourteen; next came my brother Fred, dark and handsome. I was the "middle one" and different in type from the two elder ones. I was of fair complexion, my creamy hair having won from my father the nickname of "Towdie." Younger than myself was another brother, Lester, also fair; and our youngest sister, Edith, four years old, was golden-haired and brown-eyed.

The only way we could meet the adverse situation was for all of us to go out to Illinois and make our home with an aunt, one of the sisters of my mother. My two brothers, Fred and Lester, in the course of time left Illinois and went to live with another aunt at Lea's Summit, Missouri. When I was seventeen, my sister Mary married a young farmer living in the vicinity of my uncle's farm. Edith and I went to make our home with her.

Following my brother Lester's death in Missouri, the restless disposition Fred had inherited from our father asserted itself. One day my sister Mary received a letter from him saying he was leaving Lea's Summit.

"I want to go out West," he wrote. "Uncle Stephen's cousin, Captain J. C. Lea, will start in that direction soon with his young bride with him, perhaps going to Colorado. They have asked me to go with them, and when this reaches you, I expect to be on the way to Trinidad, Colorado."

The Captain J. C. Lea whom Fred mentioned must be more fully introduced, for he and his household are an integral part of my own story.

Lea's Summit had been named for the Captain's father, Dr. Pleasant J. G. Lea, a prominent physician in the early days. Dr. Lea was a man of sterling qualities and until the Civil War cleft Missouri into two factions was held in high esteem by all. Dr. Lea's wife was from the North, a fact which made him suspect among the Southern sympathizers of that section. Mrs. Lea had returned to the North at the outbreak of the war, but that move only served to make matters worse for the doctor.

In the guerrilla fighting that was carried on in Missouri during the Civil War, a crowd of despicable cowards surrounded Dr. Lea's house, set fire to it, and shot the doctor through the heart when he came out to learn why the mob had gathered.

Dr. Lea's two sons, J. C. and F. H. Lea, were then young men of eighteen and twenty years respectively. They had hoped to remain neutral, but it was impossible to do so. The Northern sympathizers in that part of the state insisted upon regarding them as pro-Southern.

One day as the two Lea boys were gathering corn in their father's field, a squad of Kansas border soldiers came along and arrested them. The next day they, together with eighteen others, found themselves lined up before a firing squad. The officer in charge, however, was friendly to the Lea boys and, before giving the order to fire, he whispered to them:

"When I give the command to fire, you both duck and run like hell. Don't stop either, until you join the Confederates!"

In this manner they saved their lives and, realizing that their only safety lay in keeping away from that section of Missouri, they joined the Confederate Army.

They served until the end of the war in the Sixth Missouri Regiment, a part of General Shelby's brigade. When Captain Lea laid down his arms and swore allegiance to the United States of America, he put behind him all sectionalism. But he wanted to be away from Missouri; away from everything that reminded him of the bitter struggle. So he went to Georgia and engaged in railroad building and cotton planting. In 1867 he married Mrs. Douglas Burbridge, but her death some four years later left him a widower.

In 1875 he met and married a charming Southern lady, the daughter of Major Wildy of Yazoo County, Mississippi. This was "the bride" Fred had mentioned in the letter speaking of Captain Lea's going to Colorado. The Captain, however, altered his plans, and settled in Colfax County, New Mexico, just below the Colorado line.

Mrs. Lea's father, Major Wildy, had also become interested in the West. While on a visit to the Pecos Valley section of New Mexico, he decided to make an investment there. The two 'dobe houses and the several hundred acres of land that then made up the embryo town of Roswell happened to be for sale. Major Wildy purchased it all for a very modest sum. He then gave the deed to Mrs. Lea, and naturally she brought her husband from Colfax County down to Roswell, in 1877. Fred came with Captain and Mrs. Lea. He had proved himself such a capable and dependable assistant in looking after the sheep in which Captain Lea was interested, that they were glad to have him down in New Mexico with them.

Fred had been away from the rest of us for seven years. All we knew about New Mexico made it a remote and fearsome place, filled with savage

Indians, wild horses, and bad men who took delight in killing each other. Fred had begun to feel the loneliness of separation from kith and kind, and this feeling finally culminated in a letter, asking if one of us sisters couldn't come down to visit him. Mary, of course, could not leave her husband and home. Edith was thought to be entirely too young for such a long trip. So the visit came to me. But my brother-in-law viewed the matter dubiously. He took the position that it was not safe for me to go out to New Mexico and live with Fred "among those wild Indians and wilder cowboys," as he expressed it.

But his objections were overcome when Mrs. Lea herself wrote and urged that I be allowed to come. She explained that I would live with her in her home, and added that both she and Captain Lea would be glad to have a young girl with them, as girls were rare in New Mexico. She urged that I hasten my departure so that I could reach Lea's Summit in time to join Judge F. H. Lea, who was then visiting his cousin Stephen A. Lea, my aunt's husband, and make the long trip to New Mexico under his care.

It was finally decided that I should go, and I started from Illinois as soon as I could get ready. I arrived in Lea's Summit only to find that Judge Lea had left a few days before. My aunt was glad to see me, and insisted on my remaining a fortnight with her. She herself felt that I was doing a wise thing in going to New Mexico; but a great-uncle,

William Thompson, a man of considerable wealth, whom I met there for the first time, took a different view. He pleaded for me to give up what he termed my "foolish journey," and begged me to remain there with him and his wife.

"We will do everything possible to make you happy," he promised. "My wife and I are getting on in years. We need just such a young companion as yourself."

But I felt that, as I had started to New Mexico to see my brother, I should carry out the program. So I declined Uncle Will's offer, promising him, however, that I would write him in case I was not happy in New Mexico. I said to him—as I did to all my relatives—that I expected to be in New Mexico only about six months, and that I would see them all in a little while. Little did I dream that my "going out" would lengthen into a stay of three years, and result in a marriage that would make New Mexico my permanent home.

Uncle Stephen Lea put me on the train one morning in Kansas City, giving me the customary advice about not speaking to anyone on the train. His advice, I recall, was not to talk to any man, be he prince or pauper, saint or sinner. I was to take no chances.

As the train sped on its way, I began to grow both lonely and nervous. The farther we traveled across the seemingly interminable miles of Kansas prairie, the more I felt that I was headed toward the "jumping-off place." As I looked from the car window, I saw nothing but mile after mile of absolutely treeless plain, and this really frightened me. The trees I had always lived with, the trees I had loved like friends—they were nowhere to be seen. The towns, few and far between, were raw and new, and the types of human beings of whom I caught glimpses were not reassuring. They did not seem like the people I had been living among; they were almost like foreigners.

Too, I began to develop a panicky feeling, because of an unexpected complication. The conductor told me that I was on the wrong train for Las Vegas, New Mexico, which was my destination. It would only be necessary to change at La Junta, Colorado, but in my state of "nerves" this change became magnified into an ordeal. I began to feel that I was quite off the road, and likely to become lost in the great West.

When the conductor called "La Junta—change cars for Las Vegas," I looked out of the window, but saw nothing that I could call a town. All I could make out through the blinding dust storm that was raging was a large wooden building, over the door of which in large letters was the sign *Harvey House*. But I had to meet the issue, so I got my bags together and left my car. The train hesitated only long enough to let me off, then pulled out toward Denver. As the train moved away, I felt forlorn indeed, standing on the windswept platform.

"This way to the hotel, Miss," said a negro porter. "I'll carry yo' bags."

At the ticket window I inquired about trains

going to New Mexico. The next one left at midnight
—six long hours of waiting! My heart seemed to
sink into my shoes. It was impossible to spend the
interval in the waiting room of the station. I needed
rest after a long day spent on the train. So I followed the porter and my bags into the Harvey
House and took a room.

But I was too miserable to sleep. I looked back
through my life and felt that I was doomed to a
constant change of base. I viewed myself as pre-
destined to a sort of *Wandering Jew* existence. My
thoughts flitted ahead in anxious speculations
about the future. I felt as if I were alone on a vast
sea, and wondered where my next harbor was going
to be. I worried about being awakened in time for
the Las Vegas train. But time travels onward,
regardless of our anxieties. The porter knocked
on my door, and I dressed for the last sector of my
journey. The midnight train arrived on time, and
shortly I was speeding on toward Las Vegas.

When I threw up the curtain next morning, I
was astonished at the change wrought in the character of the country by just a few hours' travel. A
vast grassy plain spread out in every direction and
above it was the bluest sky I had ever seen. Cattle
were grazing everywhere, those nearest the railroad bolting away as the puffing monster invaded
their domain. An occasional herd of antelope stood
fearlessly and watched the train speed by. A few
isolated ranch houses in the distance set me to
wondering about the women and girls who might
live in them. Would I live in such a house when I

reached Roswell? Would I forego all the comforts of civilization, such as I had known during my life on an Illinois farm?

As the day wore on, I realized that the train was climbing to a higher altitude. The heavy puffing of the engine was one evidence; so, too, were the juniper and piñon trees, characteristic growth of the mountains. I knew that the end of my journey must be at hand, for I had been told that Las Vegas was among the mountains, and that to reach it I must cross Ratón Pass, one of the highest points reached by any of the American railroads at that time.

At five o'clock in the afternoon the train drew into Las Vegas. I hurried out to the platform, eagerly scanning the faces of the men standing around. Where, in this crowd of Mexicans and cowboys, was the brother I had not seen for seven years? Was he that tall, lithe figure in cowboy attire, wearing a broad felt hat, who came pushing toward me through the crowd? When the sun-browned face broke into a smile, I knew it was he.

"Fred!" I cried, and threw myself into his arms.

Tears I had stubbornly held back during the past days of anxiety and dread simply had to have free course now. Even Fred had to wipe a mist from his eyes.

"How did you know me, Sis?" he asked.

"Just by your smile," I replied. "It's the same happy smile you always had, though you have changed a lot in other ways."

And he had, indeed, for when we parted he was

seventeen and I was twelve. Now he was twenty-four and a man in the full sense, for the West and its responsibilities brought full maturity sooner than it was reached in easier environments. I knew that this figure, dressed in the fashion of his occupation—tight trousers tucked into cowboy boots with curiously pointed heels, gray flannel shirt, covered by a waistcoat merely, and a crimson silk handkerchief tied in a loose knot at the throat—was now thoroughly self-reliant and a responsible human being.

I was yet a slim miss, weighing less than one hundred pounds, my blonde hair hanging in two heavy braids down my back, tied at the ends with black ribbon. My traveling dress was a white-and-black plaid, with a broad sash of the same material. My hat was a black sailor, with a band of *grosgrain* ribbon.

"Well, Sis, I guess you want to get over to the hotel and work the dust of travel off," Fred suggested, as the train disappeared. "We can't start for Roswell until tomorrow," he added.

I looked around for a hotel, but did not see one in the row of houses extending along the street that paralleled the railroad track.

"Hotel?" I said. "Where *is* the hotel?"

"Oh, not here; it's in the Old Town part of Las Vegas. Don't be afraid. Of course it's pretty tough over there, but not so tough as this new part. We'll go to the Grand View Hotel."

Grand View Hotel! Oh, yes, I had heard of it. Captain Lea had written that, in case I arrived in

Las Vegas before Fred, I was to go to the Grand View, and he had advised the proprietor to give me his best attention. All the way on the train, when I gave way to my forebodings, I had thought of the Grand View as a sort of refuge, if I should fail to find Fred waiting for me. I had conjured up visions of it as a place befitting its high-sounding name.

But as we drew in sight of it, after driving the mile between Las Vegas (New Town) and Las Vegas (Old Town), I realized how misplaced my imaginings had been. Fred escorted me into an old run-down, two-story 'dobe building, with the plaster broken and falling from the mud brick wall, the windowpanes cracked, and in some places entirely missing. As I climbed to my room in the second story, the creaking of the rickety stairway, which was the only means of access to that part of the establishment, gave me a panic-stricken feeling. But the room I had been given reassured me. It was quite clean and comfortable.

I threw up the window to let in some of the fresh air. What a glorious panorama of mesa and mountains met my eyes, stretching interminably in all directions! Fred was in the adjoining room and I called to him:

"Brother! now I know how this hotel got its name. This is the most *glorious* view!"

"Hold onto your adjectives, Sis," he answered. "You have only begun to see New Mexico. You'll get an eyeful before long that will really require high-powered language to describe. Yes, this is a good view, but better ones will come your way, before long."

When I looked about the Mexican town surrounding the hotel, I was reminded of old scenes in Nicaragua. I felt on friendly intimacy with the squatty, dirt-roofed brown houses, with dark-skinned beings moving in and out of them.

"New Mexico!" I thought. "Yes, it must be that. After all, it's merely a part of Latin America, although a territory of the United States."

And I wondered if it would ever become Americanized.

"What a funny team!" I told Fred early next morning, when he drove up to the door of the hotel, ready to start for Roswell, in the isolated Pecos country.

"A pony and a mule—what a combination!" I laughed.

"Just the same, they're the best in the country," Fred assured me calmly, as he boosted me into the seat of the yellow buckboard. "Susie, here—" he slapped the little cowpony on the back "—can't be beaten in the whole country for a long hard drive, and this mule Pancho is the best that money can buy. You're used to seeing big draft horses back in the States! They wouldn't last a week out in this country! It takes a pair like these to cover these plains. They'll get us over the two hundred and thirty miles we have to go, in as quick time as any team you could get. They may make you laugh, now, but you'll respect them before you finish the trip."

After seating me, Brother jumped in. The
buckboard was off at a bound. Soon we were out of
sight of the town and out on the broad, open range
that stretched away, mile after mile, to the south.
Fred's tough little team settled down to a steady,
even trot that put ten miles behind us every hour.
The cool October air made my light coat feel comfortable. We talked incessantly. Fred wanted to
learn about everybody back in Illinois, and I
wanted to hear all about him, and the Lea family,
and the Pecos country, and the life there.

Fred was evidently anxious that I should not be
disappointed in Roswell and the Lea family. He told
me that Captain and Mrs. Lea had two children, a
boy of six and a daughter less than a year old. The
little girl, he said, was the first white child born in
Roswell. Then there was Mrs. Calfee, the widowed
sister of Captain Lea, and her two small boys, who
were also members of the household.

"You'll like Mrs. Calfee, for she's a regular
mother to everybody," Fred told me earnestly.
"You'll like them all, I'm sure."

"I hope so," I replied, "but what about Roswell
—is it anything of a town?"

"Well, there are just four *chozas* in the place.
Let's see—there's one that's the post office, another
is the blacksmith shop, another is the store, and the
fourth is Captain Lea's house."

I gasped in dismay at this description, for the
knowledge of Spanish I had picked up in Nicaragua
enabled me to understand that *"choza"* meant a

mere dugout. But Fred quieted my apprehension, after enjoying a quiet laugh at my expense.

"The Leas," he said, "do live in an adobe house, but it is far from being a *choza*."

The buckboard journey from Las Vegas to Roswell required five days. At the end of the first day we stopped for the night at the stage station of Anton Chico. The second night we put up at the stage station at Cedar Cañon, and the third and fourth nights at similar places. All the way down, Fred furnished me with information about the country and people. He wanted me to appear as little like a "tenderfoot" as possible, and his coaching was intended to give me advance knowledge, and the acquaintance that would make me seem a little less like a newcomer.

Of course my own questions brought on much of this. If I asked about the heavy growth of grass on the hills, that brought forth an explanation of grama grass and its value for grazing, together with an account of the two varieties of this grass— one white, the other black. Fred was so ready to impart information that he did not stop with that, but went on with an account of the manner in which the cattlemen got control of this grass. He told me all about the different sorts of "claims"—the desert claim, the homestead claim, and the preëmption claim.

"Everybody out here is after land, and a good deal of it," he said. "It takes a great many acres to furnish grazing for a herd of cattle of any size. But what counts out here is not so much the land itself, but the water. The man who controls a water right of any kind controls thousands of acres, if he wants them. Some of the settlers don't bother to become actual owners of the land. Take John Chisum, for instance. He actually owns only a comparatively small number of acres of land adjacent to his Spring River ranch, six miles south of Roswell; but he used to claim as his ranch all of the Pecos Valley, from Seven Rivers on the south to Cedar Cañon on the north, a stretch of country nearly one hundred and fifty miles long. But things are changing. Captain Lea believes in getting land rights strictly according to the land laws, and he and others are giving the Chisums and their 'right of discovery' idea a good jolt. 'Old Man John,' as everybody calls him, has seen the handwriting on the wall. He's confining himself now to a much smaller range, and he is getting valid title to the land. You'll hear a lot about this when you get down to Roswell."

"But doesn't a great deal of trouble arise, in connection with disputes about the ownership of the land?" I asked.

"You bet it does!" Fred answered emphatically. "We've had a lot of trouble over range rights. To some extent, it was a factor in the 'Lincoln County War' of a few years ago. Range rights was at the bottom of that row, although cattle stealing played a part in the trouble."

I asked if Captain Lea had taken part in the Lincoln County War. Fred said that he had not.

"You see," he explained, "the Captain had just

come into the country. That made it easier for him to remain neutral. And most of the fighting was at Lincoln, which is about sixty miles west of Roswell. But there was one time when he got himself involved in a sort of aftermath of the War. Mexicans at Berendo, near Roswell, had been mistreated by a gang of outlaws who had fought on one side or the other in the Lincoln County troubles. These men had gone into the Mexicans' homes and helped themselves to whatever caught their fancy.

"Captain Lea has always owned a very kindly feeling for the natives. So when he heard about the outlaws at Berendo, he rode over to do what he could to straighten matters out.

"But the Berendo *gente* were inclined to take Captain Lea for one of the outlaws; in fact, one Mexican had threatened to kill the next white man who showed up in the settlement. This fellow saw the Captain getting off his horse before one of the houses and he started to make his threat good. Fortunately, a Mexican named Abran Candelario recognized Captain Lea and threw himself between the two. He yelled at the man with the gun while he was throwing his arms around the Captain:

" 'This is my *buen amigo!* You can't kill him until you have killed me!'

"Of course, the Mexican with the rifle didn't dare fire at one of his own race. Candelario continued to protect the Captain until he was able to mount his horse and ride away."

This grim story made me shudder, but I was

getting too tired from the all-day ride to let it worry me for long.

One thing Fred seemed greatly concerned about was my attitude toward the men I might meet. He stressed the fact that I must not judge them by their appearance or, more important, their antecedents. He explained that it was the custom of the country to take a man for what he was at that time and place, without prying into what he had been formerly. He told me that the men all led lives of more or less hard work, and generally dressed "rough-and-ready," in a practical style that suited what they had to do. He also made plain to me that many of the men led what might be called "womanless" lives; he said that, at first, I might not understand—much less relish—their evident interest in me. The fact that I was a young woman, and a newcomer from the States, would, he assured me, attract all the cowboy eyes in that part of the world.

Fred concluded his good advice by saying:

"Now, Sis, I hope you'll try to be nice to all of them. You will find them gentlemen, in spite of some ways peculiar to the cowboy."

I remember that at the time I didn't fancy all this "brotherly counsel" on a subject which I, as a young lady, felt I understood better than he.

"Of course I'll be nice to them," I retorted. Then to show I was nettled at being so thoroughly advised, I added: "Don't you think I'm usually nice to people?"

"Why, of course," Fred assured me quickly,

"you're always nice. I just wanted to sort of 'prepare the way,' so that you won't be voted 'stuck-up' by any of them. You'll get used to their ways after awhile. Don't be afraid of any of them. Ninety per cent of the men you will meet will be gentlemen, even though they don't wear white collars on Sunday. You'll learn to like them and to trust them. Keep your dignity and self-respect, of course; but don't be 'stand-offish' with them—that's the point of all this advice."

Then, to bring me into a more agreeable mood, he added:

"Girls are as scarce as hens' teeth out here. The cowboys gobble up all that arrive. I'm afraid I'll lose you that way before you have been out here long."

Of course I had had my fears and anxieties about venturing into the West, but to be "gobbled up" by cowboys—or even one cowboy—had not been on the calendar; so I drew Fred out on some other matters about which I did have fears, namely, the fighting and the Indians. He told me of the various ways of making a livelihood he had tried in his seven years in the West—scouting for the government, running cattle, herding sheep, and a little of everything a man did in that part of the world.

"It seems to me," I ventured, "that it appears to be a place where men do a great deal of fighting. Have you ever been mixed up in anything of that sort?"

"No," he replied, "I haven't. But there are lots of men who have. Down below Roswell, near the place called Seven Rivers, there's a cemetery where they say forty men are buried who died with their boots on."

"With their boots *on?*" I asked in amazement.

"Yes, that's the expression out here. It means they died under some form of violence that did not allow them time to remove their boots. In other words, they were shot."

"Do you mean to tell me that there are forty men in that graveyard who were killed?"

"Exactly. It was like this," Fred went on. "Seven Rivers has always had a lot of tough characters there. It is just a settlement, with a post office, a few houses, and a saloon. The men only go into Seven Rivers for a 'good time.' That means they drink, and usually drink too much. Then they're ready to quarrel over nothing, and that leads to a fight—and a shooting. Card games, especially, furnish grounds for many quarrels."

"Mercy! I hope Roswell isn't a place like that!" I exclaimed.

"No," Fred reassured me quickly, "you bet it isn't. We boast we have had no killings there. The people living there represent a good class. Mrs. Lea, who owns the land on which the townsite is laid out, has never allowed a saloon in it—a regular saloon, I mean, devoted exclusively to selling whisky and letting people drink it at a bar. Captain Lea, of course, keeps whisky in his store, for it's just as much a part of the supplies as sugar or flour or gunpowder. The cowboys wouldn't work if they couldn't look forward to a few drinks when they come to town. Captain Lea sells it by the bottle or by the jug, but he won't allow them to drink it in the store. And if he thinks one of them is drinking too much during a visit to town, he can't get any more whisky that day, not for love or money!"

"I'm glad to hear that about Roswell," I remarked, "and from what you have just told me I think it must be different from other places out here."

"It is," Fred agreed. "Very different!"

"And what about the Indians?" I asked.

My ideas about "The Noble Red Man" had been gleaned from reading aloud at my uncle's such tales as *Star-Eye, the Queen of the West;* and *Sitting Bull's Revolt*, from a periodical called *Saturday Night*. Fred shrugged:

"Well, they have given a lot of trouble, all right, but that danger is getting less and less all the time. We scarcely hear of any raids now. Sometimes the Indians are unfairly charged with stealing horses and cattle when the stealing is actually done by cattle rustlers who disguise their trail by wearing moccasins. That makes their footprints serve as a basis for an accusation against the Indians. There is a reservation about eighty miles from Roswell, where the Mescalero Apaches live. But we seldom see any of the Indians in town. The soldiers at Fort Stanton look after them pretty closely and keep watch to see that they don't leave the reservation."

On the last day of this long buckboard journey, we made a very early start.

"It's forty miles from here to Roswell," Fred remarked, as we started from our camping place on the plains. "We must make it by five o'clock, if we can."

This program he was able to carry out, and in late afternoon we forded North Spring River. Half a mile farther on, he stopped the team before the wooden veranda of a square 'dobe house.

"Well, here we are!" Fred told me smilingly.

A tall, soldierly man appeared in the house door. Without turning, he called:

"Sallie! Oh, Sallie! Come see the little stranger Fred's brought us!"

He came out to the buckboard and never, so long as I live, can I forget that first sight of Captain Lea. Not until he put up his long arms to help me down, did I realize how tall he really was—six feet four. But on that first evening in Roswell, when I set foot on that friendly ground a lonely, somewhat frightened, girl "Out West," it was his kindly smile, the live, humorous hazel eyes that I noted particularly.

"Fred," he said solemnly, "we'll have to admit that, when you go on an errand, you do a good job!"

"Sallie"—Mrs. Lea—came out to meet me. She had a fair-haired baby in her arms. She looked me over, from head to foot.

"Why, what a *tiny* little girl you are!" she said. "I expected to see a tall young lady—probably because Fred is tall."

She introduced her children, Wildy and the baby, Ella. Mrs. Calfee also came out and promptly displayed that motherly instinct of which Fred had told me.

"My child, I'll be a mother to you," she promised. "I know how hard it must have been, to leave your dear ones and come all this way to strangers." Then she called her son Edgar and introduced him to me.

Mrs. Lea was a woman of medium height, with a mass of lovely brown hair coiled on top of her head. She had the graciousness typical of the women of the South. Mrs. Calfee was very much a contrast to her, in appearance. Like her brother, the Captain, she was tall and angular. Both women wore long, full calico dresses reaching to the ground, and were much beruffled around the lower edge. They did not make the least pretense of being stylishly dressed. They had been in New Mexico so long that they had lost interest in "prevailing styles." They wore what seemed best suited to their needs.

Mrs. Calfee conducted me into the house, and showed me the room I was to share with her. It was a half-story affair under the eaves.

"You will share this with the children and me," she said. "I know it is not very inviting, but it is the best we have."

"I'm sure I'll like it," I replied, although I realized it was going to be different from what I had been accustomed to in Illinois at my aunt's home, where I shared my room with only my cousin.

"I'm glad you like it," she said. "We've been rather crowded here since I came with my two boys. I came out to Las Vegas because of my husband's health. He died two years ago. Brother Joe would not hear of my going back to Missouri, and insisted that I come here to Roswell to live with him. But you are tired, Sophie, and I must not give you the family history at this time. What you need is a little rest before supper. Lie down and try to sleep for a few minutes."

And so "a little gal tenderfoot" from Illinois became an inmate of the Lea home at Roswell, in remote southeastern New Mexico.

The "Nickel-Plate Lady"

MY FIRST SUPPER at the Lea home involved a number of new acquaintances. When I entered the dining room I encountered twenty stares from as many young men connected in one capacity or another with the Lea outfit. It was highly disconcerting to face the eyes of two rows of men seated on benches extending along both sides of a long homemade table. But I felt less nervous when I saw Mrs. Lea seated at the head of the table.

"Boys," she announced to the assemblage, "this is Miss Sophie Alberding, from Illinois."

Mrs. Lea never did things by halves, and she next introduced each man individually. The "boys" did not rise, I observed, but simply acknowledged the introduction with rather bashful nods.

"Come and sit by me, Sis," Fred called out, and pushed the man next to him a few inches farther down the bench, in order to make room for me.

"Now, boys," Mrs. Lea told them with a laugh, "if I run out of boarders, I'll just have Miss Sophie sit on the upstairs gallery, where all the boys coming by can see her. Don't you think that will help fill my dining room?"

"Well," a drawling voice came out of the crowd, "I was just on the way to say, Mis' Lea, how I'd like for you to mention among the girls that I've bought two new sheepskins for my *calchon*. Any nice girl as wants to can sure put her shoes under *my* bed!"

The boisterous laugh that drawl roused deepened my embarrassment.

"Don't mind," Fred whispered to me. "The boys are always 'hurrahing.' You'll have to learn how to take it."

Then Bill—the drawler—addressed his remarks to me:

"Miss Sophie, I'm certainly going to make your feet tingle, first dance that comes along. I'm the dag-gonedest fiddler in the whole Pecos country, if I do say it myself. Now Buck, there—" and he pointed to a rather handsome young man, who colored perceptibly at the introduction, "—he reckons *he's* some musicianeer. But you just want to hear me play *Hell Over the Fence*, or *Turkey in the Straw*, or a few more."

"We'll give Miss Sophie a chance to hear you, Bill, as soon as the roundup is over," Mrs. Lea said from her seat at the end of the table, rescuing me for the moment from Bill.

I was glad when the meal was finished and the last one of the cowboys had disappeared through the door. My first impressions were not altogether agreeable. I wondered if I could ever get accustomed to these "untamed sons of the range" and their ways.

The following morning I awoke early. Hastily dressing, I stole downstairs and out the rear door, in order to inspect my new surroundings before anyone else was up to interrupt.

To the north of the Lea house was a large *acequia*, or irrigation ditch, lined with giant cottonwoods. Just beyond the *acequia* was another brown 'dobe house, with a shingle roof and small porch in front. This, I learned, was the post office and store belonging to William H. Cosgrove, more familiarly known to all as "the Don."

Looking toward the east, I could see nothing except some crimson bluffs. These I afterward learned, were the edge of the famous "Llano Estacado," the Staked Plain, of Texas, which the Rio Pecos, fifteen miles from Roswell, skirts for part of its course southward to the Rio Grande. Not a tree nor a shrub could I see in all that unbroken stretch to the horizon, where the rising sun was breaking the dark blue into red and gold. Then I turned and looked toward the west. There, too, was a similar unconfined expanse, broken by a low ridge, somewhat closer than the bluffs eastward. This was a part of "El Bordo," a rocky ridge beginning in the Panhandle of Texas and extending into New Mexico. El Capitán, the mountain I had seen the day before as I came toward Roswell, loomed blue and pointed, like old Fujiyama of Japan.

Toward the south I could see a line of trees which I later learned marked the windings of the Rio Hondo on the south and Spring River on the north. At that time both were large, clear streams, abounding in trout. Spring River rose from springs some two miles from town. The Rio Hondo had its source in the White Mountains—or, rather, was formed by the junction of the Rio Bonito and the

Rio Ruidoso, both streams originating high in the mountains.

In front of the Lea house a broad, level stretch of roadway was partly flooded by the overflow from an irrigation ditch on the south side of the house. A dozen large cottonwoods bordered the street toward the north. Directly opposite the house was a large corral with an adobe wall five feet high.

In one corner of this corral was a one-room adobe building, where my brother slept at night. His part in the Lea establishment was to act as a guard for the Captain's valuable horses at night, to prevent their being stolen.

Behind the house was another large adobe-walled corral. This was for milch cows. At milking time some twenty would be confined there, for Mrs. Lea insisted upon having plenty of milk, cream, and butter for her table. I soon discovered that among the curious features of the West, such as digging wood from the ground (as in the case of mesquite roots) and obtaining water from underground sources (as from the artesian wells) was the fact that, although it was literally a "land of cows," it was a country almost unsupplied with milk and butter.

Just south of the Lea home were a few odds and ends of buildings, all built of adobe bricks. One was a general merchandise store, another a blacksmith shop, and the third, a little removed from the others, was the home of Rufe Donahoo, the blacksmith.

After I had finished a brief exploration of my new surroundings, I went back to the kitchen to help Mrs. Calfee prepare breakfast. As I was setting the table, I overheard Minerva, the maid, talking to Mrs. Calfee in the kitchen:

"She ain't a bit stuck-up, like I reckoned she might be," Minerva said. "But her clo'es sure do make the rest of us look mighty old-fashioned. The cowboys will think she's 'nickel-plated.'"

"Nickel-plated?" What could that mean? I wondered, then decided to ask "Auntie," as Mrs. Calfee had asked me to call her. When breakfast was over and the boys had all scattered to their several tasks, I asked her what "nickel-plated" meant in the language of the cowboys.

"Why, bless your heart," she laughed, "it means the best of everything. If a cowboy can carry a nickel-plated six-shooter, or if his spurs and bridle are decorated that way, he feels as proud as Croesus. They often spend all their money for such an outfit. But what makes you ask? Did you overhear what Minerva said about you?"

"Yes, and I wondered what she meant," I confessed.

"Well, it's nothing to worry over, child. I am afraid you're destined to be called 'the nickel-plate lady'; in fact, some of the boys are already calling you that. Incidentally, you'll find the cowboys frank and outspoken. If they admire you they'll 'spit it out.' If they fall in love, they're just as likely to propose within the first twenty-four hours—if not sooner."

"But Auntie," I said helplessly, "how am I to *stand* all this attention? I've already been frightened out of my shoes. I'm not used to such ways of doing things."

"You'll have to get used to it, dearie. Why, you've made a conquest already!"

"I? Made a conquest?" I repeated amazedly. "Why, I haven't shown any partiality—unless, perhaps to that boy from Kentucky. Which one of the twenty-five boys around here are you referring to?"

"Jake. The one with the snake-bitten hand. He told me he 'shore thunk' that you 'was about the daintiest little heifer he ever done see.' Your apron helped. Jake says 'them there little aperns of hern shore do make a feller's heart go pit-a-pat.' I do believe he asked for that second helping of meat at breakfast just to have you cut it up for him."

"Oh, no, Auntie, you must be wrong," I countered. "I'm certain he'd just as soon have you or Aunt Sallie do it. Does the doctor think he'll lose his hand? I don't think Jake will ever be so silly again as to try cracking a rattler's head off, no matter how much of a bet he's made."

"No, Dr. North says he won't lose the hand, but he does think it will be a long time before the poison from the bite leaves his system. And, I think Jake intends to stick around the house and have the 'nickel-plate lady' cut his meat for him!"

A few days later, Mrs. Lea called me to come out on the front porch and be introduced to a tall, angular cowpuncher named Winchell. I recall that my first impression was that everything about him seemed to "droop." Perhaps his long mustache, which hung like a weeping willow branch, did most to create that impression, but his whole manner made me think he must be the "melancholy Dane" himself.

"Mr. Winchell has come to take us for a drive in the farming district of the valley," explained Mrs. Lea. "Get your hat, my dear. Mr. Winchell will go for the team."

Winchell was shortly back with a vehicle known as a "democrat." It was a famous conveyance in the Pecos Valley, for only men of wealth like Captain Lea or John Chisum could afford "fancy" vehicles. The farmers used wagons, and the ranchers buckboards.

As I climbed into the rig, Winchell cautioned me:

"Be mighty keerful, Miss Sophie. These 'ere hawses are wild as untamed devils. Reckon you better sit in the front seat with me."

I could not help noticing a queer smile on Mrs. Lea's face as she took the back seat with Baby Eleanor. I felt that Winchell was maneuvering the whole thing so as to have me where he could bestow complete attention upon me. I resented it, and for a moment thought I would announce my choice of seats as the back one with Mrs. Lea. Then I remembered the advice that had been given me so many times by my brother Fred, by Mrs. Calfee and others, to "be kind" to these men and their courtship methods.

It was a pleasant drive. Productive farms were beginning to spring up, now that large irrigation ditches were being carried through the fertile soil east of Roswell. Winchell explained it all to me methodically:

"Well, Miss Sophie, there's three big *acequias.* One flows from North Spring River—the one you see north of Cap'n Lea's home, but this one flows from the head of South Spring River, which is down near the Chisum ranch. The farmers call it 'Poverty Ridge.' The third ditch—it's taken from South Spring River, too—runs down by Oregon Bell's ranch and is called the 'Pumpkin Row' ditch. You sure can make stuff grow in this 'ere valley, once you git water. There's some alkali in the soil, but it washes out in a year or two."

We stopped at one of the places and bought some fresh vegetables, for, although it was October, there had not yet been a killing frost. Mrs. Lea at last remarked:

"I won't take any more this time, Sophie. You and Mr. Winchell can come back if we need more."

My chin went up several degrees. If Mrs. Lea imagined that I would make a habit of riding with this gawky cowboy—why, he was just Captain Lea's horse wrangler!

A day or so later, Mrs. Lea remarked that the mail from Las Vegas had arrived, and suggested that I accompany her to the post office. This occupied the front room of the Cosgrove house, just north of the Lea place. Besides attending to the mail, Mr. Cosgrove had a stock of dry goods and boots and shoes. His dry goods section consisted of a dozen or more bolts of calico and muslin, with an assortment of denim and corduroy trousers and flannel shirts. His "shoes" were cowboy boots for men and heavy-soled shoes for women and children.

One thing that impressed me was that everything about the place was immaculately clean and orderly. Mr. Cosgrove was himself a dignified man, and dressed more carefully than most of the men I had seen. I sensed the fact that it was these differences that had won for him among the cowboys the nickname of "the Don."

The mail was not yet "up," so Mrs. Lea busied herself looking among the shoes for something that might fit little Wildy. I was left to my own devices and began to feel uncomfortable, for the place was filling up with men, looking for their letters and papers. I was keenly aware of the eyes turned in my direction.

Presently Winchell's long, lank figure loomed up in the doorway, and I was greeted with:

"Why, howdy, Miss Sophie! Mighty glad I happened here when you did. Won't you come up to the counter and pick out a new calico dress? My treat, you know."

"You—buy me a dress?" I gasped indignantly. "You certainly won't! Who ever heard of a young man buying dresses for—for a *respectable* young lady? You certainly have the gall of an ox!"

When I had finished unburdening myself upon the astonished Winchell, I flounced out of the store without waiting for Mrs. Lea.

When Mrs. Lea arrived home shortly, she made me tell her all about my "explosion."

"You shouldn't have been so hard on the young fellow, Sophie," she said. "These cowboys think nothing of buying dresses, shoes, or stockings for the girls they take a fancy to. Winchell only meant it as evidence that he was fond of you."

"Well," I retorted, "I'm not one of his girls, and I don't want him to be fond of me, either!"

And I burst into tears.

"Of course not, my dear," Mrs. Lea said kindly, "but you can't keep him from being fond of you, or of hoping to get the advantage of the other boys by being first to be nice to you. He was dreadfully hurt by your conduct. So I told him I was sure you had misunderstood, and would be glad to accept a silk handkerchief from him. I hope you will. I explained to him that back in the States men don't think of giving clothes as presents to their lady friends."

"Well, I don't want to encourage him to be fond of me," I sniffled, "but if it pleases you, Aunt Sallie, I'll take the handkerchief."

"Here it is," replied Mrs. Lea, "his own choice."

She waved the vivid red-and-blue square before my eyes, trying to control the smile that wanted to break forth. Then she added a little lesson to me in the remark:

"The very fact that Winchell doesn't belong in your class should be reason enough for you to be polite to him."

"I suppose so," I replied meekly.

But I was a long while coming to feel other than insulted by Winchell's wanting to buy me a dress. It ran counter to all the teaching I had received. The old doctrine under which I had been brought up was ironclad—that a girl should never accept gifts other than candy, flowers, or books from any man save her affianced husband.

But there was a more particular reason. Winchell did not interest me, and I was determined not to accept attentions from him, even though Captain Lea and his wife both seemed to think I should do so. Dalton Cable, the Kentucky boy, was more interesting to me, but he did not concern himself to make any overtures for a while. Gradually, however, he began to show me more and more interest.

I heard much about the dances, and wondered when there would be one. It was a few weeks later that Captain and Mrs. Lea fulfilled the promise that after the roundup they would give a dance. After supper, on the evening it was to be held, the furniture was all removed from the dining room, and the dirt floor well sprinkled to lay the dust.

"Now they can dance all they want to with the 'nickel-plate lady,'" Captain Lea said laughingly. For that title had been settled on me by the cowboys, although Winchell had tried to give vogue to "Lily of the West" as being more "poetic."

"They won't be able to get enough girls to go around, on such short notice," said Mrs. Lea, dubiously. "Oh, that's dead easy," replied the Captain. "Barney Mason likes to tie a handkerchief around his arm and play girl. That will make another, and we can scrape up a few others here and there."

It was my first experience at a cowboy dance. The musicians were "Buffalo Bill" (not the celebrated showman) and Buck Wise.

Winchell was the first to claim a dance with me. As we stepped out on the floor, Buffalo Bill shouted:

"I'll play *Lauderbach* in honor of the 'nickel-plate lady,' because I've just been hankering for the time when I could show her how this little music box can hum."

Then he settled back in his chair in the far corner of the room and scraped his bow back and forth over the strings of his fiddle, his whole body swaying rhythmically.

Dalton Cable claimed the next dance. It was a square dance, and the "prompter," Mack Hennessey, bent his body over at an angle of about forty-five degrees, beating time with his foot and calling out: "Swing that girl, that purty little girl, the girl you left behind you." Dalton left nothing undone in the way of activity. He almost swung me off my feet as we kept time to the music. Backward and forward we went, to the tune of *The Girl I Left Behind Me.*

Barney Mason, with a bright red-and-yellow handkerchief on his arm, afforded the crowd much amusement by dancing with Buck Wise. Right in the midst of the dance, Tom Emerson, who had just arrived on the scene, took Captain Lea aside to inform him that he had no "breeches" fit for the dance.

Later he reappeared in a pair of Captain Lea's trousers. As the Captain stood six feet four, and Tom was some ten inches shorter, the seat of the trousers hung down almost to his knees. But Tom hitched them up as best he could with his leather belt.

Tom's reëntry on the scene was signaled by his calling out in a foghorn voice to Buck Wise as he danced with Barney Mason:

"Don't hug your gal so tight, Buck; 'tain't etiket, and besides, Buck, she ain't *used* to it."

A loud laugh followed this outburst.

"Swing once around and go it again!" the prompter called out, concluding with: "To your seats!"

What a happy, healthy hodgepodge it was! So different from any social gathering I had ever before attended. I began to feel less resentful of the cowboys and their attentions. But my doubts revived when the "finale" came. Buffalo Bill had resigned his place as musician and left the room. When he returned, I saw Captain Lea whisper something to his wife, which I did not overhear. Immediately, however, Mrs. Calfee came over to me. She took my hand and said in a low tone:

"Come, my dear, let's go up to our room."

I wondered what it was all about, but thought that possibly it was just their way of getting me out of the dance, for fear I might be growing tired. I was rather glad to get away, for I don't think I had ever known dancing partners who put as much physical activity into the performance as did those cowboys.

Mrs. Calfee and I hurried up the stairs and had hardly reached our room when "bang!" came the roar of a six-shooter from below, and a bullet tore through the floor and whizzed between us. I nearly fainted with fright, but Mrs. Calfee said calmly:

"Don't be alarmed, my dear; that sort of thing sometimes happens."

"What happens?" I gasped.

"Why, it's just what they call 'shooting up,' out here. Buffalo Bill got drunk, and when the news got around, we knew what to expect. That's why the dance broke up and I hurried you off up here. Don't be frightened; he won't do any damage."

The following morning, when I went down into the kitchen to start breakfast, the first person I encountered was Buffalo Bill. He was meek and penitent, and anxious to ask my pardon:

"Gosh, Miss Sophie," he said as he hitched from one foot to the other, "I sure hope I didn't skeer you last night. Reckon I was flabbergasted, or else I'd never done sich a thing. Old John Barleycorn got my goat afore I knowed it. I promise you, honor bright, it won't happen no more."

Then he added with a half sigh as he looked down at his boots, "Why, I want you to know I'd lay down my life any time for a good woman."

Bill was evidently in earnest, for he never came to a dance again under the influence of liquor.

The dance seemed to bring me more strongly

than ever to the attention of Dalton Cable. Immediately a rivalry sprang up between him and Winchell for my company, and I thoroughly enjoyed their attempts to out-maneuver one another.

"Uncle John" Chisum

THE CHIEF TOPIC of conversation at the Leas for
some time had been the new house being built on
the Chisum ranch on South Spring River. One day
a long, covered wagon passed along the road in
front of Captain Lea's, drawn by six yoke of oxen.
I watched the outfit with interest, wondering if it
were a party of emigrants or a supply of new merchandise for the Lea store. But it was neither, as I
learned when a young surveyor named Alderberry
stepped into the kitchen to remark:

"Well, I just saw several loads of furniture
going out to the new house Uncle John is building.
They seem to be putting on airs out there."

"Do the Chisums put on airs?" I asked.

"Bless you, child—no, indeed!" Mrs. Calfee
answered. "They're not stuck-up. Cowpunchers
are just as good as anybody, according to Uncle
John's way of thinking. Why, he's even having a
special room built at the back of the new house for
them to hold dances in. He's explained it by saying
that he don't intend to have his new Axminsters 'all
beat up by their hoofs.'"

Scarcely had Alderberry left the kitchen when
I heard a very loud laugh from the living room. It
was distinctly a man's laugh, loud and deep, a laugh

not merely from the diaphragm, but one that implied the whole body.

"Sophie," Mrs. Lea called, "come here and greet a gentleman who says he wants to meet the 'nickel-plate lady' he's heard so much about from the cowboys."

I dried my hands hastily and pushed back a stray lock of hair as I passed through the door. Then I was introduced to "Uncle John" Chisum. Of course I had heard of him as the very wealthy cattle king of that section. There he stood in the middle of the room with his hat in his hand, red-faced and hearty, a man of about sixty-five. He was saying to Mrs. Lea:

"Frances wanted something from your husband's store, so I just hitched the gal-mule to the buggy and come along."

Then he turned to greet me.

"Bless my heart!" he cried. "So this is the little girl I've been hearing about? I *am* glad to meet you, my dear."

Somehow I liked him instantly, as he held my small hand in a viselike grip. I realized his strong, frank personality. His dignity showed him to be a man of importance, and his genial laugh showed that he knew how to be human. He was a self-made man, who had had but little opportunity for schooling; yet he had remarkable business ability, and his opinions were valued by everyone.

Our talk was about the new house, which had now reached the stage where the new furniture was being installed.

"I wonder," Uncle John said, "if we could borrow Miss Sophie some day for a visit? You see, Frances wants some advice about them new-fangled curtains she's putting up. I thought maybe Miss Sophie might know something about it, seeing she has just come from the States."

"Why, most certainly," Mrs. Lea answered. "Sophie would like to go, I am sure—wouldn't you, Sophie?"

"Yes, indeed I would," I agreed eagerly.

For a long time I had wanted to see the new house of which I had heard so much. Carpets—hardwood floors—oh, how grand to be among such fine things!

"Well, I must be running along," Uncle John said. "Frances will be waiting for me. Little girl—" he looked at me with a twinkle in his sun-squinted eyes "—I'm right glad to know you, and I'll be over for you next week."

"Thank you; I'll be glad to go," I replied. But my woman's curiosity had to be satisfied on one matter. "Is Frances your daughter or your wife, may I ask?"

Uncle John broke into one of his characteristic laughs.

"You'll have to learn to be better at guessing. Neither one, my little tenderfoot gal. Frances is my cousin. She keeps house for me, and she has promised to stay until I get a wife."

Then he passed outside to his buggy, turning to wave his hand at Mrs. Lea and me as he drove off.

"He's awfully nice," I told Mrs. Lea. "I know I am going to like him."

"Yes," she replied, "everybody thinks the world of Uncle John Chisum."

Tuesday of the following week, Uncle John came over for me. As we drove down to his place behind what he called the "gal-mule," I could not refrain from asking "how come" he called the animal by such a queer name.

He prefaced the answer with a laugh as usual.

"Well, I reckon it's because he's the only thing on the place the women folks can drive."

I was surprised to find the new house wonderfully modern in all its equipment and furnishings. The fact that his home was two hundred miles from a railroad had not deterred Uncle John and his cousin Mrs. Towrey from providing the home with everything the East might have to offer.

We had dinner in the new dining room, and the occasion called for a certain degree of ceremony. Mrs. Towrey asked Uncle John to escort me. He offered me his arm in most gallant fashion. As we approached the well-laden table he laughed, looking at me:

"Will you be seated at my left, Mrs. Chisum?" he asked, bowing graciously as he pulled out the chair for me.

"You can tell Dalton and Winchell that their prayers are not answered," he said. Then he fairly roared, not so much at my embarrassment as at the look of consternation on Mrs. Towrey's face. Ever after that he addressed me as "Mrs. Chisum," not so much to tease me as to annoy Winchell and Dalton.

The week I spent at the Chisum place was a busy, interesting one. Although there was a Mexican girl to help with the housekeeping, she knew so little about it that poor Mrs. Towrey had to oversee it all. I volunteered to help, and one day I happened to be cleaning Uncle John's sleeping room. He was working at a beautiful walnut desk, figuring some accounts. I heard him say "this furniture and everything has cost a sight of money," and I knew this was an indication that he wanted to talk. So I asked a question that was on my mind. When I had come into the room I had been surprised to find the bed already made.

"Do you always make up your own bed, Uncle John?" I asked him.

The question provoked his usual roar of laughter.

"Why, child, do you think that, after forty years of sleeping on old Mother Earth's bosom, I could crawl into all that finery there—those spreads and pillow shams and suchlike?"

Then he pointed to a cowboy's ordinary *calchon* and a roll of blankets behind the door.

"*That's* my bed. I make it down on the floor beside that majestic affair which Frances makes me have in my room. I roll it up in the morning."

When the time came for my return to Roswell, Uncle John drove me back behind the gal-mule. As we rode along the old pioneer told some interesting tales of the heroic men of the Southwest.

"Take Captain Lea," he said. "Now, to look at him, you might not suspect that he can play the hero when he needs to. He did exactly that, once, and the Chisums will never forget it. Did Fred tell you about it? Well—it was during the cattle war you've heard about. I wasn't here at the time, but my brothers Jim and Pitser were. Some of the men who were against us planned to mutilate Pitser. They were going to capture him at Captain Lea's house, where he was visiting, and give his ears a jingle-bob slit and put a Chisum Long Rail brand on him. The 'posse' was all set for the performance. They got together back of Captain Lea's store, and tanked up on whisky; so they were all ready for anything.

"Captain Lea got wind of it through an outsider. He sent his colored boy out to the corral to get Pitser's horse, and take it secretly to the back door. Then he helped my brother to get out and mount. He instructed him to ride for his life, and Pitser certainly did. Luckily, it was a dark night, so he got away without much trouble. But it was a close call, for the posse heard his horse's hoofs hitting the trail, and sent a few shots after him. So you see why nothing at our house is too good for Captain Lea. He is certainly a fine character."

When Uncle John delivered me over again to Mrs. Lea, he said:

"Thank you kindly, ma'am, for permitting us to have the pleasure of Miss Sophie's company." Then he turned to me and added, with a twinkle in his eye, "I'll be over for you soon to make us another visit, Mrs. Chisum."

"Well, well," Mrs. Lea exclaimed, as Uncle John turned the gal-mule toward the South Spring ranch, "it seems to me that you've made another conquest."

"Why, he's sixty-four, and I'm nineteen," I retorted. "He didn't mean what he said. That's just a joke of his, to tease Mrs. Towrey. He also enjoys it because it will make it possible to have some fun with Winchell and Dalton."

Then I began to talk about my visit.

"But we did have a good time together. He asked me where he should set out the young orchard he plans to start. He also wanted to learn where I would prefer to have the rose garden. He has an *acequia* running under the porch of the open hall in the house, and every day at noon he had great fun calling out to me, 'Mrs. Chisum, it's time for us to feed the fish.'"

I described the new house, a long rambling abode, with four rooms on each side of the open hallway in the middle. Uncle John had insisted on verandas on both the front and the rear, or as I might say, on the west and east of the house, due to the fact that he could then enjoy sitting in the shade at any hour of the day, or as he put it:

"In the morning, when the sun is shining on the east side I can sit on the west side and be comfortable, and vice versa."

I explained how the place was being beautified with grass and rosebushes and shade trees. Uncle

John had told me it was costing him twenty thousand dollars. My own opinion was that the sum was not too large for a man who was rated as a millionaire.

Captain Lea was interested in what I had to tell about Uncle John's agricultural experiments. I mentioned the peach orchard, with a large adobe wall all around it, and the fact that acres and acres of alfalfa were soon to be planted. For it was Uncle John's theory that alfalfa was bound to become the mainstay of the valley. He believed the passing of the open range would mean the end of the cattlemen unless they created pastures on which to fatten stock for the market.

Captain Lea nodded and said that Uncle John was reputed to have a pretty long head.

"Maybe he knows what he's talking about. But, Sophie, what do you think of the old gentleman? Did he make love to you?"

"No," I said emphatically, trying to decide if the Captain were in earnest. I wondered if he chanced to be party to those allusions to "Mrs. Chisum." It seemed to me that this entire country was "infested" with a matrimonial bee.

Thanksgiving was the occasion for a big dance at the Chisum ranch. Everyone within a radius of seventy-five miles was invited, even to the little children, who were put to bed while their elders "danced the moon down and the sun up." The sun *was* well up before the last guest departed, leaving a trail of dust. Uncle John had lived up to his reputation and set a pace for the future. Literally it had been the "biggest dance in the country."

Soon after my first Christmas—I think it was close to New Year's—I had a great surprise in the form of a handsome present from Uncle John.

He came into the house, saying:

"Well, Sophie, if you've finished what you're working at I've got a little something for you by way of a Christmas present, even if it is a little belated. I've been expecting to hear of your wedding before this, but you must be a hard weasel to catch!"

He fumbled in his vest pocket and brought out a small box.

"Here's a trifling trinket for you," he added.

A "trifling trinket," indeed! Opening the box, I saw reposing on its white velvet lining a pair of glittering bracelets. Uncle John beamed.

"I sent to Merod & Jacquard's in St. Louis for 'em. Like 'em?"

"Like them?" I echoed. "Why, I just love them. You really don't mean they are for me?"

"Certainly they're yours! And that ain't all. Tom's bringing over a pony for you. Then you can ride over and see Frances whenever you want to."

I know I fell far short of expressing to Uncle John my appreciation of so much kindness. I felt some hesitancy about accepting such a gift from one I had known but a short time. Then I reflected that it was probably "the way of the West."

Enter John William Poe

SOME TIME IN MAY OF 1882, Milo Pierce, Captain
Lea's partner in the sheep business, mentioned an
important name in my hearing. He was talking to
Mrs. Calfee about Sheriff Pat Garrett when, in
passing, I overheard a part of their conversation.

The name which caught my attention was that
of a man famous New Mexico over at this time; a
man of whom I had heard countless times but had
not chanced to meet—John William Poe, once the
stock detective of the Canadian cattlemen and the
deputy who, more than any other, was responsible
for the death of Billy the Kid in Fort Sumner.

Milo Pierce was telling Mrs. Calfee quite casually that Pat Garrett refused to stand for reëlection, so the prominent men of Lincoln County
planned to make Poe the next sheriff.

Mrs. Calfee remarked that Poe had not been
in Roswell for a long while, and Milo Pierce explained that he had been occupied with the prosecution of Pat Coghlin, the so-called "King of the
Tularosa."

"Poe's just about finished with that case now,"
Pierce said. "I think we'll be seeing him here before
long."

This prospect interested me greatly. I had met

Uncle John Chisum and other important figures of
the territory, including Pat Garrett, but more than
any other John William Poe interested me. I had
no sentimental thoughts about him, of course. I did
not know what he looked like, even. But everything
I had heard led me to expect an unusual character.
So I waited with interest the arrival of this
celebrity.

Two weeks later Mrs. Lea went back to Mississippi and Louisiana to make a visit of several
months' duration. I "fell heir" to the major part of
the housekeeping in her absence—and this was no
light undertaking.

Captain Lea was obliged to charge a nominal
sum for meals, and make his house a sort of hotel,
otherwise he would have been "eaten out of house
and home," in the familiar Western phrase—for
Roswell was one of the stopping places between
Pecos City, Texas, on the south, and Las Vegas on
the north. Too, those going westward bound for
Lincoln, the county seat, and White Oaks, the mining town, broke their journey in Roswell.

Captain Lea was the most hospitable and gen-
erous of men. He had no thought of making a profit
from this "business" of furnishing food and lodging, but in self-protection he had decided to charge
an amount per meal which would at least pay the
cost of the food eaten by strangers.

The Captain promised me all the money coming
in from casual travelers, while that paid by his
"regulars" went into the "hotel" fund as usual.

There was an unusually large number of travelers that season, so my collections let me buy pretty dresses—very much appreciated because of the dances I attended.

Week followed week. The roundup came; the dances continued our staple form of social activity. Occasionally we went on horseback rides and picnics. Everybody went to everything. Those were the most democratic people I had ever known. Such things as "invitations" were practically unknown. It was simply the general understanding that everyone was to join in whatever good times might be abroad. I was fast growing used to the West and its ways, especially that of the men and their marriage proposals! I had considerable practice, I must admit, in fending them off, for within a space of ten months I had seven proposals from as many young men—and some of them had even passed out of the "young men" category!

One night just at bedtime Captain Lea called me into the back room. I put down the oil lamp I had just lighted, thinking that he wanted me to broil him a venison steak—a frequent occurrence.

But I saw Sheriff Pat Garrett sitting before the hearth with his long legs stretched toward the fire, while Captain Lea walked up and down. Both of these extraordinarily tall men (each was six feet four inches tall!) were very solemn.

"Sophie," the Captain said slowly, "I've just had a letter from John W. Poe, our next sheriff. He's coming to Roswell for a visit, and he'll stay here with us."

I said "Yes, sir," and waited. It did seem to me
that he was making a good deal out of John Poe's
visit to him. Captain Lea looked at Pat Garrett,
then at me again.

"Poe has been down in Old Mexico. Buying
dogies to stock a ranch he and Frank Goodwin have
just bought near Fort Stanton. Poe has been in the
hospital at El Paso. He had a bad attack of Mexican
fever."

"Yes, sir," I said again, when he hesitated.
"And he's going to stay here for awhile and
recover?"

"That's it! I think he wants to do some hunting
over on the Llano Estacado. He's been fond of that
country ever since his buffalo-hunting days."

Pat Garrett had not said a word. But out of the
corner of his eye he seemed to be watching me.
Whenever he saw me turning his way, he would
lean and look into the fire.

"Now, Sophie," Captain Lea said very slowly,
"I'm very anxious to have you like John Poe."

"Well," I told him—and I was rather surprised,
"I usually do like people, don't I?"

"Yes. Of course you do. But this is—well, it's
something rather particular. I don't want you to
like John Poe just as you like everybody else. In
fact—well, the truth of the matter is that Pat and
I have talked all this over and——"

He looked at Pat Garrett, but the sheriff was
studying his boots, now. So Captain Lea frowned.

"You see, Sophie, John Poe is going to be our
next sheriff. And he's going to be more than that:

eventually, he'll be one of the really big men of this whole section. He's a bachelor and—and Pat and I have decided you should marry him. That's what I called you in to tell you."

For a moment I was utterly dumb. I could only stare at those two amazing matchmakers. Then I exploded:

"And what gave you the idea," I demanded furiously, "that you could just call me in and tell me whom I should marry? Do you think you can dispose of me as if I were one of your prize short-horns? For if you do, I'll tell you right now——"

"Now, now, Sophie!" the Captain protested. "I'm not trying to dispose of you! I—Tell her how it is, Pat!"

"It's like this, Miss Sophie," Pat Garrett said in what he evidently meant to be a soothing tone. "You're not looking at the proposition in the right way. The Captain only means that we've talked this over and decided that it would be a mighty fine thing for you both, if you married John Poe. He's really a wonderful man; I know him well. And if you could like him enough to marry him, it would be a fine thing."

I was trying to hold in what I felt like saying. And Captain Lea took up the argument when Pat Garrett stopped:

"We're just trying to help you out, Sophie. Pat and I can't see anybody else around here good enough for you. Take Alderberry, for instance. He's a good fellow, but he's got consumption. Dalton's even worse, for he likes liquor—well, there's

no hurry about this. You think it over and take
your time. It may sound a lot better after you've
seen John Poe."

I thought I had heard all I could bear for one
night. I fairly rushed out of the room and upstairs
to my room. All that night I tried to decide what to
do—what I had to do. It surprised me that out-
siders—even so good a friend as Captain Lea—
should undertake to choose a husband for me. As a
civilized woman, I felt that it was my affair, that I
had the inalienable right to pick my own man.

Nothing further was said about the matter
until the following Sunday. I had just finished
washing the supper dishes and was putting them on
the table for breakfast, when Captain Lea came in
and stood looking at me.

"John Poe's in town," he said. "He'll be over
pretty soon. Better run upstairs and smooth up
your bangs. I want you to look your very prettiest
for him."

It was not hard to obey the order. I had no objection at all to meeting this famous John Poe,
whom everybody seemed to consider one of the
territory's coming men. I *wanted* to see him. It
was having Captain Lea and Pat Garrett calmly
select him as my future husband that I objected to.

When I came down into the living room a little
while later—coming as near to looking my "prettiest" as I could manage—Captain Lea was just
letting a tall, wide-shouldered man into the room.
They shook hands cordially. Then Captain Lea
turned to me:

"Mr. Poe," he said, "this young lady is Miss Sophie Alberding, our guest."

I am sure that I looked up into the eyes of this handsome, stalwart plainsman and realized then and there that "the conqueror of the citadel" had come. All the Alderberrys and Winchells and Daltons slipped far into the background. I remembered something Pat Garrett had said to the effect that none of the men I had been thrown with stood on the same footing with John William Poe.

Captain Lea and John Poe talked about the cattle business and the news of the day for awhile, then the Captain suggested a game of euchre. He seemed very much surprised when John Poe said he had never played cards.

"You are a curiosity on the frontier!" he said. "Ten years in the West, and you don't play cards."

"I've seen so many killings come out of card games that I never wanted to learn to play," John Poe told him. "But if the young lady is willing to teach me, I'm ready to learn now."

He proved an apt pupil. Dalton dropped in just as we commenced our game and partnered with Captain Lea. When John William (I always thought of him as that, afterward) was dealing, Dalton leaned across the table and pulled one of my braids. It was thrilling to see John William frown at that mark of familiarity!

The following week was almost an ordeal for me. John William went out on the Llano Estacado antelope hunting, and during his absence both Alderberry and Dalton "came courting" at all hours. It was as if they suspected my interest in John William and were trying to take advantage of his time away. I had so completely dismissed them from my mind that probably I was "cool." They started a row between themselves; each accusing the other of having turned me against him. So I had peace after awhile.

Then John William came back from the hunt, and Captain Lea had told him so much about my expert steak broiling that I had to demonstrate on the antelopes brought in. While I was cooking them over a mass of glowing mesquite coals, John William stood close by. After a time, he asked:

"Do you like to cook?"

"I don't know," I answered. "I never asked myself. I've just sort of gone along and done it. Captain Lea taught me to broil antelope steaks cowboy-fashion. He likes them that way, and so I suppose that's why I'm expert in that particular line of cooking."

"You do it mighty well," John William said. Then, after a minute, he added: "And while you're doing it, you make a picture any artist could be proud of."

I was so surprised at that direct compliment that I jogged the coffee pot and almost upset it. John William laughed at me and caught the tilting pot.

After the meal, the others one by one disappeared. Whether it was a preconcerted move or not I never knew. But I strongly suspect that Captain Lea engineered leaving John William and me alone. He moved his chair over to mine and asked directly:

"After I'm gone, will you write to me?"

"I—I don't know," I stammered. "I never have corresponded with men."

He laughed and moved closer.

"I'm not asking you to correspond with men. I'm only asking you to write to one man. Will you?"

I found myself very much embarrassed.

"Well," I said hesitantly, "I'll have to ask Aunt Ella—Mrs. Calfee. I always consult her, because I haven't a mother or sister here. If she says I may, I'll be glad to write you."

"Then I'll have to see Aunt Ella myself," John William told me. "For I must have some letters from the little girl who cooks such good meals."

"But everybody in Lincoln County will know about it in a week!" I said, thinking about the postmaster. "It will be spread everywhere that I'm writing to you."

"That's right," he agreed. "And I don't like my private affairs becoming public property, either. I'll tell you: Suppose you have Captain Lea address your letters to me, and I'll throw the gossips off the trail by addressing yours to him. How will that do?"

And then I saw Captain Lea's fine Italian hand! He had evidently been talking to John William, just as he had been talking to me. For a moment I was thoroughly indignant at this being "managed." Then I forgot it, for John William said:

"I have to go now, little Sophie. But before I go I'd like to tell you that I want you always to be perfectly honest with me. I'm very much attracted to you. But if there is any attachment—any reason at all—that makes you unwilling to write me, I'd like to know it now. Is there any reason?"

"Not any!" I said quickly. "I'll write to you— often, if you want me to."

During the succeeding days, I was very happy. I knew that John William cared and would go on to care more. And he was so completely the model of the frontiersman that his coming into my life in this way seemed wonderful.

One morning when the mail came in from Lincoln, the county seat, Captain Lea called me into his room and, with a quizzical expression, pointed to a letter on his desk. With the envelope held tightly, I ran up to my room and shut the door. I needed complete privacy for reading my first love letter.

"My dear little girl," it began, and went on to say how much he desired my friendship. He did not want to supplant someone else in my affections. He hoped that I was free to listen to him and he would anxiously wait for my reply.

That was the tenor of the letter, and I could read between the lines of rather formal sentiment the real emotion that had moved him as he wrote. I ran downstairs to find Mrs. Calfee.

"Aunt Ella!" I cried. "Oh, Aunt Ella! He's the grandest man in the world—John Poe, I mean."

She smiled at me affectionately, if tolerantly.

"Yes, he is a good man, my dear. A very good man. And you mustn't trifle with him as you do with these boys here. *He* wouldn't bear that for a minute."

Our correspondence went on for some time, Captain Lea addressing all my letters to John William, and his letters to me coming addressed to Captain Lea. And in the Roswell post office there were some comments to the effect that Captain Lea and John Poe must "have a big hen on," because of the number of letters they exchanged!

And more or less to avert suspicion, I continued to drive with Alderberry or Dalton Cable. The feeling was strong that John William would not be pleased to have me going with men who wanted to marry me—and any woman will understand that this was not altogether an unpleasant feeling. . . .

Then a letter came from Lincoln which said that John William would be coming down "just as soon as possible; to say something very important."

And a local event hastened his visit. For John William had been elected sheriff, and he policed Lincoln County with a firm hand, if with a wide understanding of frontier men and frontier ways. It was like this:

Roswell was different from almost every other frontier town I have heard of, in that Mrs. Lea owned the townsite and could say what should or should not be.

One of her restrictions governed saloons. She had never permitted an outright drinking place to be operated in Roswell. Captain Lea's store always contained a barrel of whisky, for it was recognized that cowboys wanted liquor and would get it somewhere. But there was an ironclad rule at Lea's that no man could buy more than a single quart of whisky in a day.

For the most part this rule was accepted by the travelers and the cowboys without any objection. But occasionally we had the "bad man" who insisted on doing exactly as he pleased. And George Griffin, a hard case (and a cowardly braggart) from the Texas Panhandle, was one of these.

He had drifted into town with a partner whose name Roswell never learned. One night the two began a drunken spree, and when the liquor they had was drunk they came down to the Lea store and ordered Dalton Cable and Dick Lawton to open it up and get them more whisky.

When Cable and Lawton refused, Griffin and his friend shot out every light in the building and riddled a display of new Stetsons that Captain Lea had put into the big front windows. Then they came galloping and yelling over to Captain Lea's house. They sat their horses outside and threatened to shoot out every window in the place if the Captain did not bring out the keys to the store.

Captain Lea was at home, with my brother Fred and Alderberry. The Captain ordered all the lights blown out and silence kept inside. This infuriated Griffin and the other man and they rode around and around the house, shooting their pistols into the air. Captain Lea told the other men not to shoot unless Griffin and his partner carried out their threat to fire into the windows.

"We're all right behind these adobe walls," he said. "But if they shoot into this house, knowing that women and children are here, shoot them straight through the heart!"

Mrs. Lea had not returned from Mississippi, but Captain Lea's widowed sister-in-law, Mrs. Edwards, was with us with her two small children.

When we heard the shooting and the whine of bullets, Mrs. Edwards picked up her baby boy and crawled under a bed. Her little daughter and I hid under another bed.

Griffin and the other man continued shooting for perhaps a quarter of an hour—though the time seemed endless to us. They galloped around and around the house, yelling curses at Captain Lea and threatening to blow the door down. Finally, they went pounding down the road toward the Rio Hondo. Griffin was too drunk to sit his horse and was thrown at the bridge. The fall knocked him senseless.

One of John William's local deputies made up a posse of cowboys, and they went out after the pair. They found Griffin unconscious on the floor of the bridge and tied him up like an Apache papoose. When he was lashed from head to foot with lariats, they brought him back to town and threw him on the floor of the blacksmith shop. Next morning he was glad to pay a fine of fifty dollars for disturbing the peace and get out of the neighborhood as quickly as possible.

John William heard the story next day, when the mail buckboard rolled into Lincoln. He was not content to let a scoundrel of the Griffin type escape so lightly. So, making a combined pleasure-and-business trip, as he said, he came to Roswell immediately.

I had no expectation of seeing him so soon, and had gone driving out to the head of Spring River. We were on the road west of town, and on the way to Lincoln, and Alderberry had just presented me with a beautifully bound copy of Moore's poems. He had bought the book in Santa Fé for me and insisted that I accept more than the book. I told him as diplomatically as possible that, while I liked him very much I could never love him. And while we were both silent, watching the sunset, I heard a horse's hoofs on the road.

Almost before I could turn, John William was beside us. He looked at me, then at Alderberry, and there was not the slightest sign of pleasure in his face!

He said something to us about being happy to see me looking so well; and being glad to meet Alderberry again. Then he touched the rim of his hat and spurred toward town in a cloud of dust.

My heart was pounding—actually pounding. I could not see why Alderberry didn't notice and guess the reason. But he didn't; in fact, nobody in Roswell even suspected the direction of my love affair until the night before my marriage, so well did Captain Lea and John William arrange matters.

That night I made myself as attractive as I knew how to do. For intuitively I knew that John Poe had come from Lincoln on that "important matter" he had mentioned; and there was no doubt in my mind that this was to me the most momentous evening of my life.

"I'll wear my blue ribbons," I thought. For I recalled vividly how he had said blue ribbons against blonde braids were lovely.

At last I was dressed and ready to go down-stairs. I went slowly, but when Captain Lea met me and looked down with head on one side, I felt a little less nervous. For he said:

"Well ... I think you'll do. ... "

Nothing of importance was said by either John Poe or myself during dinner. But when it was over and we sat talking in the living room, discussing the two drunken cowboys, he looked at me more than at Captain Lea, to whom he was speaking.

"Griffin and the other fellow oughtn't to have got off with just a fine," he told the Captain emphatically. "Thirty days or more in jail is what that type needs—and what they'll get, if I put my hands on them! I'm sorry they had got away before I reached Roswell. I'm going to show some rowdies of the Griffin stripe a pair of handcuffs!"

"I don't doubt that you're right," Captain Lea agreed. He got up. "You'll excuse me? There are two or three important letters that I have to write."

Mrs. Lea had come back from her visit. She had been sitting with us. Now she got up, also, and smiled at us.

"Time to put Baby Eleanor to bed," she told us. "I'll say good night to you, Mr. Poe."

And so John William and I were left alone. He drew a chair close to his own and waved me to it.

"Well, little girl," he said. "And what have you been doing all this time?"

I was embarrassed, and it was strangely hard to talk.

"I think I've told you everything in my letters. Everything, that is, except——"

"Except what?" he interrupted, frowning. "What have you done that you didn't tell me?"

"My pony had to be shot," I told him weakly. "Fred was riding her, and she fell and broke a leg. So he shot her——"

"Oh!" John William said. "Is *that* all? Are you —sure there's nothing else you haven't told me? *Sure?*"

I nodded and he smiled across at me.

"I'll give you a riding pony. In fact, I'd like to present you with all the horses on my ranch. I will, if you'll give me the right. If you'll marry me...."

And there it was—what I had expected, and still it was not what I had expected. Rather, I had not known what it would be like, merely by anticipation.

"You should know that I love you," he said slowly and earnestly, and with a note of tenderness in his voice that I had never heard before. "I know very little about women. My life has been spent mostly among men. You have a great deal to teach a man like me. Will you marry me? Can you promise?"

I nodded, and his arm came around me, and he lifted my face to his for the first kiss.

There was so much to talk about that evening. ... And we managed to discuss a great many details of our marriage. The only thing John William insisted upon was having it soon.

"I've spent most of my life on the range," he told me. "I've missed a lot. And now that I've found the girl I want, I'm certainly not going to waste any time in putting her in my house—our house. Here's what we'll do: I'll send to St. Louis tomorrow, to get the engagement ring. You can wear it here with the family for the time being—not outside, where everybody will notice it. Then we'll get married as soon as we can settle whatever has to be done——"

"I'll get my *trousseau* together," I agreed. "It needn't be a long time, if you want it soon."

And that was the way John William proposed and was accepted, in the spring of 1883.

And So I Was Married

MARRIAGE IN THE SOUTHWEST of 1883 was very frequently one of the makeshifts of the land. It could hardly be otherwise, when within a radius of three hundred miles of Roswell there was not a minister, not even a Catholic priest!

Among the Mexicans this was considered a small deficiency and unimportant; many of them became "man and wife" to all effect without troubling at all about the blessing of a priest or the sanction of the state.

But among the Americans there was a strong tradition governing marriage; it was felt that marriage was not valid unless performed under the laws of the church or state, or both. And since there was no simple way to obtain a minister, five justices of the peace, scattered over the enormous county of Lincoln, handled almost all the weddings.

I may leave consideration of my own marriage for a moment, to consider that of Mrs. Calfee, which preceded mine. She had managed to hide from me her interest in Milo Pierce, of whom I have spoken before as Captain Lea's partner in the sheep business. But on an afternoon in late October it was made plain to me. For while we were resting in our room under the eaves, I heard an unusual commotion outside. I looked out and saw a bunch of

cowboys working with a team. They were struggling with the unbroken horses, swearing and yelling as they tried to get blindfolds on them.

Milo Pierce on his crutches was hobbling around
the group. He had been shot in the leg some time
before and was still considered a cripple. While I
watched, the cowboys got the broncos blinded, and
Pierce moved up to the wheel.

Then I called Mrs. Calfee and told her excitedly
that Milo Pierce was going to drive that unbroken
team—a performance a whole man might have
dodged. She ran over to the window and when
Pierce was helped into the seat she began to cry.

I turned to stare at her. Even though Milo
Pierce was like a member of the family, being Captain Lea's partner, Mrs. Calfee's show of feeling
was surprising.

Pierce settled himself with the lines, and the
cowboys jerked off the blinds. The team lunged,
and the wagon rolled forward. As far as we could
see them, the broncos were kicking and fighting the
harness. Mrs. Calfee leaned from the window, saying over and over:

"He'll be killed! He'll certainly be killed!"

But presently the wagon came in sight again,
returning. The team trotted as quietly as a pair of
old buggy horses. And Mrs. Calfee wiped her eyes
and faced me.

"Of course you're wondering," she said, "so I'll
tell you the secret. Mr. Pierce and I are going to be
married, and when I saw him get into that wagon,
with that crippled leg—but it's exactly the sort of

thing he would do. And I admire him because he's like that."

She told me a great deal about him. To her, he was a "diamond in the rough" but a genuine diamond. And for the first time I heard a certain page of Lincoln County history. For she told me what nobody else had mentioned, the story of Milo Pierce's wound, a sort of aftermath of the Lincoln County War.

He had been a leader of the small cattlemen in their battle with the ranchers who owned great herds and monopolized water rights. After the "war" was over, some of the warriors held grudges. There was a man named Bill Jones, whose ranch adjoined the Pierce-Nash outfit, and who remembered all the old scores of the fighting.

He came over to Pierce's one day and in the course of "talking cow" began to make threats against a man named Beckwith.

"Beckwith is a good friend of mine," Pierce told him quickly. "A very good friend of mine. I won't listen to talk like that about him."

Jones persisted in vilifying Beckwith, and he and Pierce were soon engaged in a bitter argument on their own account. As Jones rode away he shifted in the saddle and yelled back:

"He may be a friend of yours, but I'm going to kill Beckwith on sight!"

"If you do," Pierce promised, "I'll kill you."

Some time after roundup, Bob Ollinger—that same long-haired deputy sheriff who was to be murdered the following April by Billy the Kid in

Lincoln—rode by the Pierce ranch and stopped to talk. Pierce was lying on a cot in his shack. The two men talked of range affairs for awhile, then Ollinger said casually:

"Too bad about Jones getting Beckwith, wasn't it?"

Pierce jumped up from the cot.

"Jones got Beckwith? Then I'll make good on my promise. I'll get him!"

But Ollinger checked him.

"No use rushing out to find him, right now. If you do, your nerves won't be steady enough. Keep cool about it. Your day will come to get him, all right."

Pierce, who had just come in almost exhausted from a long, hard ride, sat down again. Ollinger went on talking and not even thought of his friend's death could keep the tired Pierce from dozing. Ollinger, in telling the story, remarked that it was a case of the old proverb about speaking of the devil and seeing him appear, for suddenly the doorway of the shack was darkened, and he looked up to see Bill Jones standing there.

He said Jones walked into the room and shook hands with him, looking at the drowsing Pierce all the time. Then Jones moved toward the bed and drew his six-shooter as he went. Ollinger jerked out his own pistol and shot Jones dead. But the bullet was almost fatal to Pierce, as well, for it passed through Jones's body and lodged in Pierce's hip. He was compelled to go East for months of treatment in hospitals and sanitariums.

It was after Milo Pierce's return to Roswell that he became engaged to Mrs. Calfee. And when the marriage was being arranged as to details, the "customs of the country" gave the pair a great deal of trouble. They had decided upon my friend Alderberry as the justice of the peace who would marry them. A date was set, and Mrs. Calfee was ready to "march down the aisle."

But Alderberry, the only justice within sixty or seventy miles, went to Santa Fé on business. And there he fell sick. Days passed; weeks went by. Still Alderberry was an invalid in distant Santa Fé. The wedding date came, and when it was certain that Alderberry was not going to appear, Pierce and Mrs. Calfee went to Captain Lea.

They had decided to drive sixty-odd miles to Seven Rivers and have the justice there perform the ceremony. But this was 1883 and there were such things as conventions (as I must have made clear in telling of my own experiences with gentlemen who came courting). Captain Lea put his foot down solidly on that scheme.

"You'll do nothing of the sort!" he told them. "My sister is going to be married right here in my home. You can wait, Milo. And so can you," he said to Mrs. Calfee. "Neither of you is exactly a young person, but your age doesn't give you any license to travel to Seven Rivers together. Not even to get married."

And when "the Big Chief"—as the family called the Captain—set his foot down, he was never disobeyed.

So they settled themselves to wait for Alderberry. And at last he came back to Roswell. But
when the new date arrived, Pierce failed to show
up. He was out counting some sheep and he couldn't
stop in the middle of the work! Mrs. Calfee fidgeted,
and the invited guests were tense—and at last Milo
Pierce came hurrying in, and the long-delayed
ceremony was performed.

It was then that I organized the first important
"musical affair" in Lincoln County. Mrs. Lea had
sent back East for what was known as an "organette." It was about the size and shape of a carpet
sweeper and it played paper rolls like those used in
a modern pianola. After the Pierce-Calfee wedding, I got Alderberry and Dalton Cable to help and
we pasted the ends of all our music rolls together
and went out to serenade the couple.

I recall *Old Black Joe* and *Kentucky Home* and
O Susanna and other songs of Stephen Foster in our
collection of organette rolls. It was something very
unusual to Roswell people, to hear those tunes
played by anything but guitar and fiddle and banjo.
We serenaded the "happy pair" very thoroughly
with the rolls joined and one of the two men constantly at the crank of that queer little musical
instrument.

My own wedding suffered no such strains and
delays as Mrs. Calfee's. In fact, when the time came
there was almost no warning and perhaps that was
simpler and better.

There had been no exact date set, but I was
ready, for I knew it would not be long delayed. So,

when John William appeared most unexpectedly in Roswell, early in May, insisting that I marry him immediately, only a slight illness made the plan impossible at the moment.

He was quite logical about it. He had been called to Seven Rivers on a murder case and, after arresting the murderer and sending him on to Lincoln in custody of a deputy sheriff, he had decided to come by Roswell and take me back to the county seat with him.

"Court opens in a few days," he told me. "I have to be there at nine o'clock, Monday, the seventh. And it will be several weeks before I can get away again. It looks like now or—not exactly never, but too long."

He would not take no for answer. He went to Mrs. Lea and asked if we couldn't be married the next day, which happened to be a Friday. She said instantly that I wouldn't think of being married on a Friday, considered an unlucky day.

"Then how about Saturday?" he persisted.

"All right," she told him, throwing up her hands. "If Sophie feels well enough, I suppose it can be Saturday."

Then he came to me and explained that it was a long two days' journey by buckboard to Lincoln and he must leave Roswell not later than Saturday forenoon.

So I was married. May 5, 1883 was the date, and the time in that early-rising land was five in the morning.

Judge Stone had succeeded Alderberry as jus-

tice of the peace, or I should have been married by a
man who had courted me.

The Leas supplied a notable wedding breakfast
—baked ham and fried chicken and hot biscuit and
candied sweet potatoes and whatever the limited
stock of their frontier store contained. I hardly
noticed the guests but I do remember Fred, my
brother, whispering that we were sixteen at the
tables. That total must have included almost everyone in Roswell.

My trunk was strapped on the buckboard. John
William picked me up and set me down on the seat.
Goodbyes were over. The sun was going higher in
the sky, and we had forty miles of rough road
ahead, the first lap of our journey to Lincoln.

From the crest of Six Mile Hill I looked back
over the village which had been my home on the
Southwestern frontier. On the whole, my days in
Roswell had been happy. I realized that the friend-
ships formed, with the Leas and others, were real
enough, strong enough, to endure for a lifetime.
Then we began to round a curve in the road, and the
tiny town slid out of sight. I kissed my hand and
looked away from the old life, looked forward to the
beginning of a new life with this tall man who sat
beside me driving Dandy and Jim.

That noon we ate lunch beside a narrow stream.
During the afternoon the scenery grew more interesting than it had been for the first thirty miles
west of Roswell. On the left was the gash in the
hills which indicated the deep gorge of the Rio

Hondo. On the right El Capitán loomed in its customary purple haze, but changing form from the pyramid I had always seen to a long range of mountains. Directly ahead were the foothills of the White Mountains.

Some thirty miles out of Roswell we began to descend a long, steep hill, and I was divided between alarm and delight, for the hill seemed dangerous, but the view below was enough to make me forget fright. Hundreds of feet below, the Rio Hondo wound like a shining serpent through the valley, nearing that gorge through which it must flow before reaching the open country, passing Roswell, and going on to pour into the Pecos.

The buckboard jumped from one level to another, and John William told me casually that the hill was "called two miles long" but added that the horses knew their business. It was like going down a stairway, but when I watched the team holding back and picking their footing, my alarm vanished.

It was wild and impressive country, amazingly different from the neighborhood of Roswell. Along the banks of the Hondo the adobe houses of the farmers—Mexicans, for the most part—were set before small orchards of apple, peach, and pear. Cottonwoods were green near the irrigation ditches.

It was easy now to understand the enthusiasm I had heard expressed by visitors to the Lea house, for this "Upper Section" of Lincoln County. And it was literally the "upper part," for Roswell was only thirty-five hundred feet in altitude, while this valley of the Hondo was a thousand feet higher.

When we passed Mexican houses, it became clear to me that my husband was a Personage. There was always some Mexican urchin to yell:

"Es el oficial mayor!"

Which would translate, roughly, that the sheriff was an important official.

And John William passed the time by telling me about the Mexican population of the Southwest, their respect for an officer, and their peculiar—and primitive—ideas of law.

Not many killings among the Mexicans, he said, were premeditated, their murders rising usually from quarrels and sudden outbursts of temper. He had dealt with only one case in which a Mexican planned a murder because it would profit him.

"That was up at San Patricio," he said. "You know the Mexican idea about sex relationships. They don't bother much about ceremony, but cut through to practical considerations. In this particular case a man and woman made a sort of common-law arrangement. She would live with him for five years. At the end of the time he would give her fifty head of sheep and forty cows. The whole community knew of the arrangement, so when at the expiration of the period they agreed to separate and she was shot while she sat at the window of the house, the neighborhood was aroused. The peculiarity of the situation was that they came down in a body to me, at Lincoln. They wanted me to go hang the man without delay. And they thought I had the authority to do what certainly seemed to be the correct thing."

He told me of other, similar cases—of men who came to him and asked calmly for divorces. One, who spoke a little English, wanted a "separate."

I told him of the case we had recently known in Roswell, where a Mrs. Curtis had filed suit for divorce and wanted to remarry before the decree was granted. Against legal advice, she proceeded with her marriage to a man named Bartlett. My friend and ex-suitor, Alderberry, was ready to marry the couple when John Rowley, one of John Chisum's cowboys, walked in on the service. He knew about the advice that Lawyer Clyde had given Mrs. Curtis and he yelled:

"Hey! You-all can't do this without a license. Mr. Clyde told you so."

"And what's Clyde got to do with my marrying?" the groom demanded. "Who does Clyde think he is, anyway?"

"I don't know," Rowley admitted, "except he's the man what makes out the licenses. But seems like he ought to know."

Even Alderberry was at a loss about the proper procedure. Finally, someone had a happy thought. He suggested that Captain Lea be consulted. So Rowley went to find the Captain and he came back all smiles:

"All right," he announced. "Go ahead with the knot. Captain Lea says you can. Says he'll stand good for it."

We had talked so much about the "original citizens" that the miles slid by without being noticed. But John William knew where he was going. He turned aside from the main road and drove up to a long, rambling adobe house that sat two hundred yards from the highway.

"August Cline's," he said to me. "Here's where we stop tonight."

A dozen bony dogs ran out and began barking furiously. A tall, bony German came to the door.

"Long time no see you, Sheriff!" he said cordially.

"A long time," John William agreed. "And I've done something since you saw me last. I've got married. This morning at Roswell. And this is my wife."

"You don't say so?" Cline beamed. He came out, rubbing his hands together and smiling. "*Mein Gott!* Married—undt ve don't know you efen haf der sveetheardt!"

He called to the house, without turning from us:

"Hi! old Vuman! Come out *pronto* undt meet mit der Sheriff vife."

A Mexican woman of unusual height shambled out. She was no less cordial than August Cline himself. She put out a hand to me and invited us into the house, telling me all the while that Sheriff Poe was her *buen amigo*, her very good friend.

They showed us into a room with ceiling of white canvas and walls tinted with a gypsum whitewash much used by the Mexicans. There was a comfortable poster bed and a quaint Mexican *olla*, or water jug, on a stand.

I shall always remember the supper the Clines served us. The table was homemade and covered

with red oilcloth, but there was milk toast and a
native steak fried to a turn and potatoes boiled
"with the jackets on" and that rare article in the
cow country, fresh butter. The hospitable Mexican
wife of August Cline filled and refilled our plates
until we had to protest.

Married Life In Old Lincoln

NEXT MORNING, early, we were again in the buck-board, beginning the last lap of our journey to Lincoln. The valley of the Hondo was noticeably narrower, and the hills surrounding it steeper. Trees were more numerous, too. Juniper and piñon began to make their appearance.

We covered the twenty or twenty-five miles from Cline's to Lincoln by noon. I had looked forward to my first view of this historic old settlement. I had heard much about the place and how it had been the scene of many bloody encounters since becoming the county seat in 1869. But I was really taken aback at its small size. The one street of the town stretched its crooked length for a mile along the south bank of the Rio Bonito, walled by squat, flat-roofed adobe houses. Some less pretentious structures, called by the Mexicans *jacals*, were scattered on the outskirts of the settlement.

As we approached from the east, I tried to get as much of a bird's-eye view as possible, but could only define this single, winding street, flanked on either side by trees.

John William smiled at me.

"Well, how does the county seat of Lincoln impress you?"

"Well," I answered, "I certainly can't call it a metropolis!"

"Hardly! The census gives seven or eight hundred population, and we have about a half-dozen stores, large and small." By this time we had come to the edge of the town, and all I could see were the rough houses of the poorer element, made of poles stuck in the ground and smeared over with mud.

"But surely," I said, "you have better houses than these?"

"Oh, yes," replied John William, "those are just Mexican *jacals*. Señora Otero, who will do your washing, lives in that one over there."

A little way beyond the Otero place, John William turned the buckboard into a gateway and brought the horses to a standstill before a neat adobe house.

"Journey's end," he said. "Let's go in and see if Mrs. Ellis can give us room and meals until we can arrange to begin housekeeping."

His knock at the door was answered by Mrs. Ellis. She showed genuine surprise at sight of me, but only said:

"Why, Mr. Poe! Where did you come from?"

"From Roswell," John William replied, "and I have brought my wife."

Mrs. Ellis barely permitted me to acknowledge the introduction before she continued:

"Goodness me! You didn't tell me to expect anything like this, or I'd have had things all fixed up for a bride. But come right in, both of you."

I could see no reason for Mrs. Ellis' concern, as everything about the place, both inside and out, indicated that the housekeeper knew her business and attended to it.

"Well, my wedding was a surprise to me, even, I might say," John William explained to her. "But I've been interested in this young lady for some time. So as I came by Roswell, on my way from Seven Rivers, I simply stopped, in a sort of now-or-never fashion, and made her marry me. So here we are, and the important question now is, can you give us a room, with board, for a month? By that time we should be able to establish ourselves."

"Of course we can," Mrs. Ellis cried. "There's Pa coming now."

"Pa" (whom I later knew as Isaac Ellis), a bearded man, was coming up from the field in his working clothes. He came around to the front of the house and greeted us cordially. I was pleased to see how friendly everyone seemed toward John William, and how genuinely they congratulated him on bringing home a wife. It augured well for my reception in the town—I thought—that everyone seemed to be counted as his friend.

Court was to open the following day, so Mrs. Ellis was beginning to have her hands full with the large crowd that always came to Lincoln at that time. But she put herself to extra trouble to give us a comfortable room. It was clean and cheerful. The bed was covered with a bright patchwork quilt, and the pillows had starched pillow shams embroidered with red thread. The floor was covered with a red ingrain carpet. In the window, through which the bright sunlight poured, hung a flower basket filled with growing gourd-ivy that trailed down to the window sill. It was the sort of room that radiated happiness and good cheer.

Our wedding was as much a surprise to everyone else in Lincoln as it was to the Ellis family. John William's most intimate friend was his deputy and jailor, J. Smith Lea, a cousin of Captain Lea. Smith, too, was "completely flabbergasted," as he expressed it, when he learned of our marriage.

"So that's your system," he told John William sarcastically. "Never hint at your plans—not even to your deputy. Just leave me in charge, but don't tell me anything."

With opening of the spring term of district court, Lincoln became a bustling place. "Main Street" was lined with buckboards and saddle horses and the mule teams which the Mexicans preferred. Lawyers from Las Cruces, even from as far away as Santa Fé, came in. In most cases they were accompanied by their wives, for the social life of Lincoln was quickened at each of the semiannual terms of court, held in May and November.

During the day interest centered in the court proceedings, but at night the absorbing matters were dances and other social festivities. "Court time" was, in fact, a general holiday. Everybody was expected to have a good time. The dances were attended not only by the Americans, but by the higher class of Mexicans. The officers from Fort

Stanton, nine miles away, added a dash of color
to the occasion.

The Rio Bonito, along which Lincoln's one street
ran, was a mountain stream carrying little water
during the dry season, but tending to become a
raging torrent at times, especially when the snows
were melting on Sierra Blanca—White Mountain
—a peak more than twelve thousand feet high.
Blanca was usually snow-covered from the middle
of November until the last of April.

The stream was bordered on each side by mountain cottonwoods, box elders, and various sorts of
underbrush. Wild grape and clematis helped to
mat all this mass together in the summer until it
was an impenetrable tangle.

Like all streams in that section, the river was
a rivulet crooked enough and, in consequence, the
bordering street had such a serpentine outline that
a person standing at one end was unable to see
farther than 'Cipio Salazar's house on the south
side. The remainder of the town came into view
only when one advanced to the turn of the road in
front of the Salazar house.

Enclosing the town on the south side were the
rather steep foothills and mountains, covered
scantily with cedar and juniper trees, and most
plentifully studded with rocks large and small.
Across the Rio Bonito was a fertile, mile-wide valley, intensively cultivated. This land was divided
into many small tracts, and most of the farmers
lived in Lincoln and went forth daily to work their
fields. But not all; against the gray of the Capitán

foothills splotches of brown adobe marked the permanent residents who had built on the ground.

Lincoln was a famous old settlement when I went there as a bride in 1883. When one had "learned" the two sides of the single street, the county seat was an open book—and one never to be forgotten.

On the north side, starting at the Ellis house, one walked almost to the middle of town, encountering but few buildings. Then there was the house where Mrs. Alexander McSween lived, after the McSween house had been burned during the Lincoln County War and her husband had been killed by Bob Beckwith's shot.

Beyond this house a round *torreon*, or rock tower, made a landmark. The tower had been built two and a half stories high by the first Mexicans to settle there. In that day, before the American Civil War, the Apaches were constantly raiding in the neighborhood. So the Mexicans kept a watchman stationed on top of the *torreon*. His saddled horse was ready in a room below him. With the first sight of Indians, he was to drop down to the ground and mount, to ride out into the fields and warn the people.

Still on the north side of the street, but beyond the *torreon*, the Tunstall-McSween store yet stood, but since the hectic days of the Lincoln County War, the building had passed, by a curious play of fortune, into the hands of James Dolan, who was a leading spirit in the "party" antagonistic to the McSween faction. Down the street, perhaps a hundred yards, was the hotel which Ben Ellis, son of Isaac Ellis, built on the site of the McSween home which had been burned by the "Murphy Posse" during the Lincoln County War. Farther west sat the old Wortley Hotel, the first built in Lincoln.

On the south side of the street houses were closely built. Just across from the Ellis home several squat adobes housed the Oteros, the Pichacos, and the Cisneros. Beyond these the old *campo santo*, the burying ground, was almost a chapter in itself of local history.

This ground had been used for burials since the earliest days of the town, and in 1883 was well filled with graves. Perhaps the most discussed grave was that of Manuel Trujillo, said to have been Lincoln's first settler and, for a long time, the leading resident of the town. His grave was made outstanding by a large stone. According to tradition, the great rock required twelve or fifteen yoke of oxen to draw it into position. Before his death, the old man had stipulated that his grave should be covered with this particular stone, and his wishes had been carried out by his friends. Some said he had done this in order to prevent any desecration of the grave by marauders. Others gave his request a religious coloring, because old Trujillo was said to have been a devout member of the queer sect of *Penitentes*. But whatever the motive, his marker was the most notable in the old cemetery.

At the time of my arrival Captain Saturnino Baca had just finished a new adobe house. The Bacas were among the *gente fino*, the "fine people," of old Lincoln. The Captain himself had made a military record in the Civil War and, shortly after being mustered out, had taken a wife from over toward Socorro.

Señora Baca was a woman of parts who not only ruled her own family like some Doña of Old Spain, but also dominated the social life of one segment of the town. Her daughters, commonly spoken of as "the Baca girls," were among the prettiest señoritas to be found in New Mexico. The only son of the Bacas, "Bonnie," had been educated at Notre Dame, a distinction that had come about when Major Murphy (he who had ruled the town so long) made young Bonnie his protégé. During *El Corte*, the court session, Señora Baca kept open house for members of the bar and others who might be in Lincoln at the time. To enjoy the hospitality of her home was a prominent feature of Lincoln's court life enjoyed by many of the most prominent men in the territory.

The house of 'Cipio Salazar had its own distinction in being the only two-story house in town. 'Cipio was acknowledged to be the finest dancer in the settlement, and at the *bailes* he was a great favorite with all the ladies. He was distinctly on such occasions what can best be described as *"un hombre muy caballero"*—a very gentlemanly man.

A bit farther to the west, on the same side of the street, were the old Patron and Montaña stores. In the latter was the assembly hall of the town, largely used for the *"big bailes."* No other room in Lincoln could have accommodated the crowds which gathered on one of those occasions. Señora Montaña and Señora Salazar were inclined to dispute Señora Baca's right to the social throne of Lincoln. It would be difficult to say which of the three appeared at the *bailes* displaying the most dazzling jewelry or the heaviest and most costly silks.

Next on the south side of the street was the newly erected Catholic Church. The town had managed for perhaps twenty-five years without a church edifice—a fact which speaks eloquently for the religious state of the section!

Just beyond the church was a residence outstanding because built of stone, when almost every other building in Lincoln was of adobe. This was the new home of James Dolan, into whose ownership had passed the McSween store directly across the street.

Next to the Dolan place, J. Y. Thornton owned a small but attractive home. Thornton, an ex-soldier, had settled close by the home of Jim Brent, John William's chief deputy, and married one of "the Baca girls."

There were no more important buildings on the south side of the street until the western limit of the town was reached. There stood the two-story building which was by all odds the most "imposing" in Lincoln, the Murphy, Dolan & Riley store building, owned by the county and made to do duty mainly as a county building, though pressed into service in other ways not strictly official. Colonel "Mickey" Cronin, for example, in 1883 rented a part of the ground floor and operated a store there. Some of the upstairs rooms were set aside as living quarters for county officials—notably the sheriff.

By the middle of June, John William and I were keeping house in the upstairs portion of the courthouse. The rooms intended for the sheriff had been arranged for our use.

Isaac Ellis freighted over from Las Vegas the set of furniture we had bought. I felt very proud of our bedroom suite, made of black walnut, the bed high and massive, the washstand and bureau equipped with heavy white marble tops. The carpet was a Brussels, with a pattern showing roses. The windows were curtained with white lawn material. This equipment was considered the last word in bedroom furnishing, in those days. As a matter of fact, we were considerably ahead of the rest of the community, for few homes in the place could equal the elegance of our bedroom in its furnishings.

There was one feature of the new home which I did not enjoy. The back stairway, up and down which I had to travel many times during the day, was still stained with blood, a grim reminder of the day two years before, when Billy the Kid had shot and killed his guard, James W. Bell. Bell had been climbing those stairs and his body had fallen to the bottom of them.

Our bedroom was the front room upstairs which Major Murphy had built for his own sleeping quarters. This had secured additional notoriety, as being the room which had held Billy the Kid after the young outlaw's conviction and sentence at Mesilla for the murder of Sheriff Brady. It was from the east window of this room that Billy had shoved out a shotgun, in April of 1881, to murder Deputy Bob Ollinger.

Below us lived Colonel "Mickey" Cronin, a retired army officer who had settled in Lincoln. The Colonel was a stout, red-faced Irishman and a particular friend of John William. Like most Irishmen, he believed in ghosts and other manifestations of the supernatural, and the old building did much to satisfy his interest in such matters. On more than one occasion he came rushing upstairs in the small hours of the night, and wakened us to announce that Major Murphy had "been up to his old tricks" again. Usually these "tricks" consisted of visiting Colonel Cronin's room, turning the bookshelves over and spilling the books all over the room.

"I didn't see him," the Colonel invariably would say, "but I could hear him walking about the room. Then I heard him steal downstairs."

Strange to say, when John William went with the Colonel over to his room, he would find the shelves down and the books scattered about the floor, just as the Colonel had reported.

As I had little fear of ghosts, I was not uncomfortable in the creepy old building. My greatest anxiety was the safety of John William. Lincoln County was then as large as one of the Eastern states, and the sheriff had long journeys to make to the four corners of the county where lawlessness occurred. I was in constant fear that from one of these excursions after murderers or other types of lawbreakers he might be brought home to me "feet first."

In midsummer certain indications set me to sewing. For several weeks I made baby clothes under the direction of Mrs. Ellis. But as I did this, I did not cease to take an interest in the life of the neighbors in the town, especially the Mexicans. They were a people so different in many ways from the Americans that I never tired of studying them. Their quaint customs reminded me of the happy days I spent as a child in Nicaragua; and the uniform respect and love they held for my husband, "*El Oficial Mayor*," naturally increased my friendliness for them.

One day my native laundress entered the room with a woebegone expression. She was usually so light-hearted that the change was startling to me. Taking her brown hand, I asked in Spanish:

"What is the matter? Why are you so sad?"

"Oh," she wailed, "my poor son Bonifacio has received the calabash. None of the girls will marry him. He will never have children. *Ay de mi!*"

And I learned one of the curious ways of courtship among these people. If a youth wanted to marry a girl, he sent her a present. If the parents favored the suit, he received an invitation to come to the house; but if not, she was made to send him a "calabash," a squash. Bonifacio had just received his calabash, and his poor old mother was heartbroken.

I did my best to console her by saying that there were many girls in the vicinity, and he would surely be able to find a wife. He was then only twenty, and when I assured his mother that no American young man would consider himself doomed to bachelorhood for the rest of his life just because one girl wouldn't have him, she was considerably consoled.

A few weeks later, when she came to deliver our clean, well-ironed clothes she was radiant. Bonifacio had found a little girl, eleven years old, who was willing to marry him at once! Would the Señora Americana be so good as to come to the wedding breakfast?

Two weeks later, I was awakened at early dawn by a volley of shots. I waked John William and he listened, then said sleepily:

"Only a native wedding, I guess."

He explained that on such occasions all the male friends of the groom brought their guns and, after forming two lines at the bride's home, from the gate to the house, discharged their firearms to frighten away any evil spirits that might interfere with the happiness of the bride.

After breakfast I went down to Mrs. Ellis', and we went together to the little adobe house where the wedding festivities were in progress. We were received with vigorous hugs from the bride's mother, according to the usual Mexican custom. We congratulated Bonifacio and his poor little bride, whose wizened face had been powdered with wheat flour until it looked positively ghostly, in spite of the dark lines of tan which her tears had washed from her eyes to her chin. But if the noise and jabbering and demonstration meant anything regarding "happiness ever after," joy was to be hers.

So, in Lincoln, I saw both their joys and their sorrows. One case I recall was extremely sad. I attended the funeral of a woman who had died in extreme poverty. The corpse lay on a bare table in the chapel while the priest chanted a mass. There was no casket, no flowers—only a worn, gray blanket covering the table on which the body rested. Candles burned around the improvised bier, while a few mourners sat around the walls of the room. When the priest had finished, four men rose and, taking hold of the corners of the blanket, bore the corpse to a farm wagon which waited just outside the door, to bear the body to the *campo santo*. The Montaña boys, who furnished music for all the *bailes*, tuned their violins at this point and began to play *Kitty Wells*, and other folk songs, with an occasional dance tune interspersed. To the accompaniment of such music, the procession moved slowly toward the cemetery.

As the time for the coming of my baby drew nearer, I began to feel great concern for myself. With John William away from home so much, I feared that when the crisis came, I might be alone. My anxiety was intensified when I realized how ill-provided with proper facilities for a maternity case was the section where I lived. I thought of Mrs. Anderson, the wife of the wealthy owner of the

Diamond A Ranch. At the time of her confinement, the only midwife obtainable was one of their cowboys!

While living in Roswell, I had seen Uncle Jimmie Farrell drive headlong into town and draw rein before Captain Lea's gate.

"Where's Dr. North—quick?" he shouted at me as I went out to see what he wanted. "Mrs. Anderson's going to have a baby, and there's nobody home but Anderson and a cowboy!"

A Mrs. Edwards joined the doctor in making the posthaste journey up from Roswell to the ranch, but when they arrived, a lively little boy greeted the doctor. When the latter inquired who had supplanted him professionally, he was told that Mr. Anderson himself had assumed the role of doctor, while George Harvey, the cowboy, had been pressed into service as "head nurse."

Mrs. Anderson had planned to go to Roswell for the occasion, but it was earlier than was expected. She found it embarrassing to have it happen as it did, but she was able to look on the humorous side of it.

"It makes me smile now," she told us afterward, "when I think of George sitting by the fireplace holding that naked little mite to the fire as one would have held a soap bubble."

It was all well enough to remind myself that if I were called upon to undergo an ordeal like that, I must view it as one of the hardships that befell women of the frontier in the early days. It was also well enough to recall the remark that behind every brave man was the heroism and bravery of a mother. Nonetheless, I suffered a great deal of anxiety while I was by myself, during the last weeks before confinement. Finally I decided that I *must* go down to Roswell and remain with Mrs. Pierce until after my baby was born.

During the last week in January, 1884, John William came down to remain with me through the ordeal. It came near causing my death. All one Saturday night in February, Dr. North sat beside the bed, stroking his chin and shaking his head.

"Not one chance in a thousand," was his verdict.

Captain Lea suggested sending to Fort Stanton for one of the army surgeons. And Dalton Cable, one of my old admirers, volunteered for the long drive which must be made at breakneck speed. Once again the buckboard mode of conveyance proved of importance in my life—perhaps I should say *to* my life.

Taking the best pair of horses in Captain Lea's stable, Dalton started at noon. He stopped at the Diamond A Ranch for a change of animals, then raced toward the fort. At Picacho, August Cline contributed his best team to the cause. At Lincoln, James Dolan, routed out of bed, assisted Dalton by "hooking up" his ponies. When Dalton reached the fort, he found the surgeon unable to leave because of a similar maternity case there, but he was glad to help out Dr. North by sending back some instruments by Dalton that would be helpful. Without stopping to rest, Dalton started back on the seventy-five mile drive. Exactly twenty-four hours after he had started on his errand of mercy, Dalton drew rein at Mrs. Pierce's. Possibly I owe my life to him.

Half an hour later Dr. North announced to John William that he was the father of a son, and that I would probably live, although it was doubtful if the child would survive. And it did not. My tiny bundle of humanity breathed uncertainly for a few hours, then went back into the Unknown, February 4, 1884. . . .

For many days I lay very ill and weak. I remained in Roswell until the first week in March, when John William—who of course had been obliged to leave me and go back to Lincoln—came down. He had Captain Baca's spring wagon, as the best substitute for an ambulance Lincoln could afford. Being altogether too weak to sit up during the long drive home, I lay upon a bed of soft blankets in the bottom of the wagon and made the trip without slowing my convalescence.

A Cabin on the V's

AFTER LIVING in Lincoln for a year, John William bought a tract of land about fifteen miles southwest of Fort Stanton. We moved out to the new location, which he had named the VV Ranch.

It was hard for me to leave Lincoln. I had been happy there, and even though the place to which I was going was our own property, I dreaded the loneliness of ranch life.

I remember how I said goodbye to the county seat. On the banks of the *acequia* behind the old courthouse was a fringe of black willows and cottonwoods which was my retreat when I wanted to escape my room. Before leaving, I went out with my needlework to the quiet nook, where heavy Bermuda grass formed a soft seat.

I sat there for a long time, sewing, thinking of my experiences in New Mexico. I had been there perhaps an hour when I was roused by the sound of hoofs on the gravelly bank behind me. It was Manuel Trujillo driving the dairy cows up to the Ellis house. Manuel mirrored his Andalusian ancestry in his ability to turn his thoughts and feelings into songs. Now, before he came up to me, I heard him chanting to himself the events of the day. When he caught sight of me, he continued singing, merely including me:

"*A ya esta una mujer baja el árbol*—there is a woman under the tree!"

Early the next morning, John William brought the buckboard around to the front of the courthouse and I climbed in behind the sturdy horses, Dandy and Jim, for another buckboard journey of great significance in my life. Soon we were driving southward, bound for the new home on the VV Ranch.

For some distance the road bordered the lovely Rio Bonito. The melting snows from the White Mountains had colored the clear water of the stream a darker shade than usual. All kinds of wreckage floated in the swift current, and the banks showed that the stream had been "on a rampage" while the water was high.

Ten miles from Lincoln was the noted military post of Fort Stanton, which had played such an important part in the history of that section. Established before the Civil War, it had served to curb the Apaches infesting the country. "The Military" —to use our local designation—had also given invaluable aid in subduing lawlessness among the civilian population. The post was attractively located in the very heart of the mountains. On one side towered Sierra Blanca, about twenty miles away; on the other, El Capitán, perhaps slightly farther. The buildings were strongly built of stone, as well they might be, for the Mescalero Apaches, on their reservation only some twenty miles distant, were a turbulent set. This military post, and the mode of life of its officers and their families, had always seemed to me, in the desert, an "oasis," representative of civilization and its ways.

As we rode on, the hills rose higher and higher. The juniper and piñon trees—always sure signs of the mountains—became more and more noticeable. After seven miles more, the road crossed an open glade which John William spoke of as the *ciénega.* Presently he pointed out a low, flat-roofed log cabin.

"Well, there is your new home, Sophie. I see John Dyer has the coffeepot boiling for our first meal."

"How can you see the coffeepot from here?" I asked him, with a laugh.

"Why, I can see the smoke curling up from the kitchen chimney, and make my own deduction."

Then he added, with great tenderness:

"I hope you will like the place, little girl. I had it cleaned last week. It's not any too spacious, but we'll add another room or two in the course of time. Anyhow, it's our own home."

When the buckboard came to a halt before the wide gate, a tall young man appeared to open it. He had been watching our approach from the door of the long low shed in the corral.

John William introduced me to John Dyer.

"It's a good thing you like the name of John, my dear," he told me. "For we have four Johns here—myself, John Dyer here, and later you'll meet John Crouch and John Ricker. Ricker claims to be the champion fiddler of these hills."

"You ought to have named this the John Ranch, instead of the VV," I told him.

"No," John William said tolerantly, "VV is a good brand, and the ranch naturally takes that name. You must know that cattlemen generally name their ranches either after their brand or their earmark. Our neighbors, over toward the Carrizozo, mark their cattle with an iron rod, a running iron, in the figure of a square, with also a straight line—or bar, as it's commonly called. Consequently, their place is called the Bar-Box Ranch. Your friend John Chisum preferred to name his ranch after his earmark, so he calls it the Jingle-Bob Ranch."

I had been hearing the expression "earmark" for a long time. I did not understand what it meant.

"The Chisum earmark," John William explained, "is made by cutting a split through the lower part of the ear, almost back to the head. This piece of the ear hangs down and bobs as the animal moves. This suggested to the first Chisum cowboys a jingling bell. My own earmark is a slash on the right ear and an underbit on the left."

He drew it for me in the dust—like the drawing below:

"I chose the VV brand," he went on, "because while it's simple, at the same time it's hard to alter. Those are the two requisites in a good brand. Every

cowman prefers a brand which can be made with a
plain iron rod, for that saves carrying a heavy
'stamp' branding iron to make a special device. My
cowboys can brand VV with four strokes of the
running iron."

As I stood in front of my new home, I owned a
feeling of utter loneliness. To live five miles from
the nearest neighbor, with my husband absent
much of the time on his official duties as sheriff,
made me sure that I must often be lonely.

But as I looked around, I admitted that for sheer
beauty of surroundings the VV could hardly be
surpassed. The *ciénega* that lay close around the
cabin was like a green meadow. Close to the ranch,
hills covered to their crests with piñon and cedar
invited climbs. Grama grass grew so thick and
high that it almost hid the fat cattle grazing upon it.

If I must be alone, it could hardly be in a lovelier
spot, I thought. Then I went into the cabin, and
once more something like dismay came to me.

It was so small, so bare! A room on the north,
another on the south, with the kitchen between; all
so low that even I, barely five feet two inches tall,
could stand upon a chair and touch the ceilings.
Each room had but one window.

There was some consolation in the fact that,
being a log cabin, there were floors of wide pine
planks, as contrasted to the hard-packed dirt floors
of most adobes in the country.

Each of the living rooms had its Mexican fireplace in a corner, and the kitchen boasted an excel-

lent wood-burning range with large reservoir for heating water.

My dining room was furnished with a long homemade table and eight "store-bought" chairs, The frontier table was always much larger than the family concerned might need. Mine must always be provided for guests; I would feed every cowboy within a radius of twenty-five miles when it pleased him to drift in from his riding.

In the bedroom we had our only "luxury"—that suite of black walnut bought for our Lincoln housekeeping.

John William watched me examining the new home. And presently he picked me up and kissed me.

"It doesn't look like much, I know," he told me. "But I hope you'll be happy with just this for the time being. Eventually, when we make our stake, I'll build you a house and furnish it with everything you want."

I realized that work was going to be my salvation on this frontier ranch, so I began at once. The house was immaculately clean, for John William had brought out a Mexican couple from Lincoln, and they had even given the walls a coat of gypsum whitewash. I had only to rearrange my scant furnishings and begin a routine of housework.

After I had settled in the cabin, the most interesting breaks in the natural monotony came with the wandering Indians who were frequent visitors. We saw not only Mescalero Apaches from the neighboring reservation, but Pueblos and Navajos as well. These last wandered down from the vicinity of Santa Fé, peddling fruit, which was always welcome in southeastern New Mexico in those days.

The Indians were always friendly, never doing us any injury or abusing any privileges we granted them. My first nervousness at sight of them quickly disappeared, and presently I would allow them to come into the kitchen and cook on my range.

The Navajos and Pueblos wore clothing of manufactured cloth with a blanket thrown over their shoulders. The Mescalero Apaches wore leggings and moccasins of buckskin and clung to their long hair, wearing it in two braids with the ends wound with strips of red cotton cloth.

They clung to their traditional garb for as long as the government would permit, stubbornly resisting all attempts to change their mode of living or their style of dress. When officials persisted in "modernizing" them they would run away from the reservation and hide out in the hills until hunger forced them back to the Agency for supplies. They were particularly attached to their braids. Like Samson, the Indian seemed to feel that courage and strength were proportionate to the length of a man's hair.

While virtually all of these wandering aborigines were courteous in their own way to me, I had one thorough scare from an Indian. It was on a bright, sunny day when all the doors and windows stood wide open and I was alone at the house. While I worked at my morning housekeeping I heard a gruff voice behind me.

"Hello. Hello."

I whirled, to face a big raw-boned Apache who stood motionless, staring about the room. I do believe that my hair actually stood on end. For just two weeks before a couple of Apaches had stopped on the Rio Bonito at an isolated cabin. They had stripped it of everything they fancied and threatened to scalp the woman who was there alone—just as I was this morning. She had broken away and run three miles to the safety of a neighbor's house. And all this flashed through my mind as I gaped at the big buck. Then I tried to appear unconcerned and asked the Indian what he wanted. In good Spanish he asked if there were any men on the place.

I said as steadily as I could manage that I would call my husband. But something told me that I was not impressing the Apache in the least. So I pointed to the door.

"My husband is *el oficial mayor*, a big chief," I told him. "You had better go away—*pronto!* For if he finds you here, he will arrest you."

He only grunted at that, but he did go outside. I ran to the window and saw him cross the yard to another buck sitting on a stump. They talked for a moment, looking toward the house. So I ran to the door and slammed it shut. I locked it and, not content with that, snatched the big table, and pulled it across the opening. I piled chairs on top of the table, then caught up one of John William's rifles and threw a shell into the chamber. I leveled it at the Indians across the window sill. They were walking toward the house now, and my hands shook. But I was determined to shoot at them.

Then John Dyer appeared, walking from the corral toward the kitchen. The Indians ran for the brush and as for me, I let that rifle fall with a thud to the floor and dropped to the planks for fear I would faint.

John William was furious when he heard of the incident. He sent word to Major Llewellyn, then in charge of the Mescalero Reservation, that if the agent did not put a stop to the Indians' leaving the Reservation on these pilfering expeditions, some of his charges would be arrested and jailed. The warning proved effective, for I never saw another prowling Indian around the VV.

During the whole of the first summer on the VV, I seldom saw another woman. My nearest neighbors lived five miles away across Eagle Creek. Pat Garrett had a place up the cañon, about the same distance, but Mrs. Garrett, a Mexican woman, spoke very little English. I had forgotten most of my Spanish, and a fluent or interesting conversation with her was difficult under the circumstances. So I didn't receive much pleasure from visiting her. My usual companions were a large shepherd dog and a big tomcat who was always present when the dog permitted him to join our company.

On days when I suffered from loneliness, I would call the faithful dog and climb to the top of one of the high hills in front of our cabin. From that elevation, the country for many miles around unfolded itself before my eyes. Although not a human being would be in sight, yet the stillness and beauty of the scene were comforting. I felt that I understood how Eve must have waited for Adam to return from a hunt. After an hour or two spent upon the hills, from which, literally, "came my help," I would hurry down the steep slopes, fortified for the hours and days ahead.

One day late in the summer, John William came home leading a dun that owned a heavy dark tail and mane.

"I bought him for you, darling," he said, as he presented the animal.

I admired "Dave" immensely, and John William told me that he had bought him from a Lieutenant Davies at Fort Stanton. The Lieutenant had been ordered to another post and was anxious to dispose of his favorite horse to someone who would treat him kindly.

I patted the lovely arched neck, and Dave put his head down and rubbed my shoulder, as though he understood that I was an appreciative mistress.

Dave was indeed a remarkable horse. His unusual beauty was not his only good point. He was kind and gentle, with a power of understanding which was almost human. We did become great comrades, and I had many a ride on his back over the hills. He seemed to sense the situation and to adapt himself to it in the fullest degree. If I wanted to scale a steep and rocky hillside, he made the effort; if I wished to loiter in some spot, gathering wild flowers, he waited patiently my pleasure.

The horse was but one evidence of the fact that

John William was trying to protect me from the loneliness which so often made ranch life a burden to women. Somewhat later, he made me another present that showed the same solicitude. He had made a trip to Kansas City with a load of cattle, and when he returned, he brought with him a Swiss music box playing twelve tunes.

"I selected this particular one," he explained proudly, "because it plays that song you sing so much—that one called *Only a Pansy Blossom.*"

It was a beautiful instrument, and although its range was almost absurdly narrow compared to a modern phonograph or radio set, yet we never grew tired of those twelve tunes, played in the soft, sweet tones produced by such an instrument.

During the winter months the employes were more often around the ranch. Johnny Patton, the cook, was especially helpful in keeping away loneliness. He was a bald-headed Irishman, owning a world of good humor and wit which was constantly manifesting itself. He had been in the country a long time and knew a great deal about Lincoln County happenings.

One occurrence which he particularly liked to describe was a fight at Blazer's Mill, on the Mescalero Reservation. Patton had been employed at Dr. Blazer's sawmill in 1878 when "Buckshot" Roberts, a cripple, singlehanded, "took on" a party of ten or twelve of the McSween warriors, among whom were Dick Brewer, Billy the Kid, Frank Coe and his cousin George, Jack Middleton, Charley Bowdre, and others. The little ex-soldier and ex-Texas

Ranger thoroughly whipped the McSween crowd and ran them from the scene, leaving their leader, Dick Brewer, dead from one of Roberts' bullets. Johnny Patton had been called upon to knock together the two coffins in which Dick Brewer and Roberts (who died the next day from a wound) were buried.

Pat Garrett was always an inveterate practical joker, and when Johnny first came to the ranch, he became a victim of one of Pat's pranks. Johnny had never been much of a horseback rider, and when he had to go out on the range with the cowboys one time, Pat schemed it so that old Tortilla, a rather mettlesome animal, should fall to Johnny. Pat and his companion Noah Ellis rode on a little in advance of Johnny and his steed. Suddenly they heard a howl from the rear, and—as Pat told the tale—when they looked back, Johnny was several feet up in the air, but evidently coming swiftly downward. They turned and hurried back to Johnny's relief. By the time they reached him he was lying upon the ground with his feet and face toward the heavens above.

"I told ye the dom' critter would scatter!" Johnny exclaimed as he picked himself up and started toward the chuck wagon.

With the coming of the second spring of our stay on the VV, I began to escape from the loneliness. John William's partner, F. M. Goodwin, moved his family from Mobeetie, Texas, to the ranch. Although they established themselves in a house two miles from our cabin, on a location near the head of the *ciénega*, their coming gave me a feeling of having neighbors, which was a great relief after my loneliness of more than a year.

Shortly after we settled on the VV, my brother Fred had come out to ride range for John William. Although his work took him away from home during the day, yet he was always home nights. This was a great comfort to me, for John William was often away on the long trips which his duty as sheriff entailed. But later, Fred was taken away from me, for he went over to the Salado, ten miles distant, to hold down a claim for John William. This made it impossible for him to be much with me.

But a great improvement was pending. A letter came from my sister Mary, asking if I would care to have Edith, a younger sister, come out for a visit. I could hardly get an affirmative answer dispatched quickly enough, and I looked forward eagerly to her arrival.

Fred went to the railroad to meet her, as he had done in my own case when I came out. But instead of going to Las Vegas, as he had been obliged to do then, Fred went to Socorro, for by that time the Rock Island Railroad had reached that place. As he had not seen our baby sister since she was five years old, and as a brief calculation revealed to him that she would now be eighteen, Fred wondered how he would be able to recognize her. He finally decided that she would have the same brown eyes and golden hair he remembered so well. He also trusted to familiar family features. These proved safe guides, for although two young ladies stepped from the train, he recognized Edith instantly.

Fred was a born tease, and his life in the West had increased that tendency. Although he was very glad to see Edith, he couldn't refrain from teasing her. He took her to the hotel to let her rest before starting on the two-hundred-and-thirty-four-mile drive to the VV Ranch, and went away for awhile. When he came back, he sat down in a splint-bottomed chair by the window.

"Come sit on my knee, Edith," he said, "the way you used to do when you were just a little tow-headed kid."

When she had responded to the invitation in a sisterly way, and they had spent several minutes discussing the family back in Illinois, Fred said:

"Well, little girl, I'd better go now. I've got to find your brother. He ought to be here by now; and he'll be glad to find you such a winner."

Edith's indignation may be better imagined than described. She "told him off" in no uncertain terms.

Her indignation only served to encourage Fred. He explained solemnly that he was a close friend of Edith's brother, and said that Fred had asked him to meet her.

"Don't cry," he said, "I'll find him for you."

Finally, he told her that he was only joking, and convinced her that she hadn't been bestowing her affections on a stranger.

But he couldn't resist the temptation to tease her. She was the sort of a tenderfoot who naturally invited that sort of plaguing. When they reached the VV, after four days of hard buckboard driving, he pulled up before our door.

"I guess we'll tie up here for the night," he announced as he threw the lines around the whip-socket. "This is Pat Garrett's place. This team has made two hundred and thirty miles in four days, so I guess they're ready for a rest."

But I "spilled the beans" that time by running out to greet Edith.

I led her into the cabin, and when she had laid her hat on the black walnut bed I pulled her over in front of the window to take a good look at her. Edith was unquestionably beautiful. Her mass of golden hair, and her luminous brown eyes made her unusually attractive. Then I looked at her lovely white hands, and instinctively I thrust my own—coarsened with work and climate—under my apron. Recalling my own experience with the men I had come among in that "womanless" country, I felt sure that Edith would simply play havoc with the hearts of the cowboys in our neighborhood.

Edith, in her turn, looked me over critically.

"You surely do look out of date," she said at last. "I guess you've lost all track of the styles, since you've been away off out here. Your back is too flat. I'll have to fix you up so you will have some style to your clothes."

"I wish you would," I accepted the offer gratefully. "But in this wilderness I haven't thought much about clothes. Somehow, you make me feel terribly old-fashioned." Then, observing a large "protuberance" at the back of her dress, I asked curiously: "What on *earth* is that funny hump on your back?"

"Why that's my bustle!" she explained.

"Bustle?" I repeated. "Why it feels to me like newspapers."

"Certainly it is. And *Globe-Democrats* at that. In Illinois, we prefer our own make to the wire ones they sell in the stores. We can make them any size we like; but the bigger they are, the more fashionable."

"Well," I said, "if there were any newspapers on the place, I'd use them for reading. I don't suppose that, out here, I've *seen* as many newspapers as you've put in your bustle. Don't be surprised if I steal your bustle while you're asleep to read the latest news from the States."

"Well, Sister," Edith announced, "I'm going to try to scrape up enough newspapers to make you a bustle before your husband comes home tomorrow. I wonder what he'll think when he sees you decked out in the latest feminine fashion!"

Next day John William came home. I ran out to the gate to greet my husband and announce that Edith had arrived. John William turned back to his saddle and began to unfasten a bundle from the cantle.

"Here's something I brought you girls," he said. "I got them at Ozane's store in White Oaks. He'd just got in a lot, and he said all the girls were wearing them. I don't want my girl and her little sister to be behind the style."

"Oh, my prophetic soul!" I thought, as I began to unwrap the package then and there. "It will be bustles!" And it was.

I ran in to show them to Edith, who was at the door waiting to greet the big brother-in-law whom she had never seen.

Edith, I noticed, seemed to have trouble fighting an inclination to laugh all the while that John William was in the room. When he had gone out to care for his horses, she turned on Fred.

"Another yarn, you scalawag."

"Now then, what's the joke?" I demanded. "Has Fred been up to his tricks again?"

"Yes! He told me particularly that I mustn't laugh at your John William's thick Irish brogue. Fred said he was terribly sensitive about it."

I had to laugh at that picture.

"John William's great-grandparents did come from Tipperary, and he's very proud of his ancestry. But the family lost its brogue long and long ago."

Edith found ranch life too drab and tame. She met a number of the cowboys, but did not encourage any of them to go farther than mere acquaintance-ship. She was "Eastern" to the core, nor the type to fit into the West. But the real cause of her indifference to our men was the fact that she had left her heart behind in Illinois. So, although she was pleasant to all the new acquaintances, she found none who could take the place "of the boy she left behind her." So, early in the spring of 1885, she persuaded Fred to take her back to Illinois. Fred returned from "the States" and went to work for Richard Hudson, in Lake Valley, New Mexico. He was killed there by cattle-rustlers the following January.

One of the last incidents I recall of my life on the VV concerned the young army officer who afterward became Commander of the A. E. F., General John J. Pershing. About eight miles from our ranch was the old Dowling Mill, one of the landmarks of the country. Frank Lisnet and his wife kept a sort of tavern there, where travelers from Lincoln to Mesilla usually stopped for the first night. The long dining room at their place was a popular place for dances, and I liked to have Edith go there. Sometimes I accompanied her, but usually I pressed Fred into service, although he, like most men in that section, scorned dancing, saying *he* couldn't see any pleasure in "prancing around" to a fiddler's tune.

On one of our trips to the Lisnets, I heard Mrs. Lisnet relate her experience with those three young lieutenants — Pershing, Penn, and Paddock — whom August Cline always called the "Three Green Peas," because all of their names began with the letter "P" and they were such utter tenderfeet.

The Green Peas came down from Fort Stanton to the Lisnet neighborhood to hunt deer.

In broadest Irish brogue, Mrs. Lisnet told how "Leftinant" Pershing shot one of the Lisnet pigs, believing it to be a ferocious wild boar. She accused him of killing the pig, knowing it to be hers, and of planning to pass it off at Fort Stanton as a wild boar "because thim fellers at the fort'd niver know the difference!"

Lisnet persuaded her to let Pershing off without paying for the pig.

"He's a grand officer, Mary. I wouldn't give a dom' if he killed the whole herd."

In 1885, John William sold the VV Ranch to a wealthy Scotchman named Cree, who proposed to develop a cattle ranch there on an extensive scale. The Crees had plenty of money, and the transfer was made through an agent named Captain Kirby. It was said of Kirby that all he was capable of doing was to hang around Santa Fé, wearing a fur overcoat, and signing checks on the Cree funds. Mrs. Cree came of a Scotch family, noted as breeders of Black Angus cattle, and it was her dream to introduce them into New Mexico, despite the fact that the Lord never intended that the Black Angus should ever do much walking. The Crees had several head shipped over from Scotland. As the cattle could not be driven from the railroad out to the ranch, they had them transported in wagons from Socorro, the nearest railroad point.

The Crees tore down the cabin in which I had lived, and used the timbers and lumber to build in part the houses which they needed for their headquarters. They came out to live in New Mexico, bringing with them the belongings of an Edinburgh family of wealth, and they preserved many of the customs of the old country, especially those by which much ceremony was made of meals.

Never having contacted people in the more advanced society to which the Crees belonged, the ranchers around took exception to all their "style," thinking they were a "proud lot" who wanted to "lord it over them." Consequently, they were far from popular with the neighboring cattlemen and their families. This feeling was carried to such an extent that threats were made against the life of the son, James Cree, who thought it "the better part of valor" to return to Scotland. The father later passed away, and after some years Mrs. Cree also returned to the homeland.

Lincoln County Lawlessness

BEING SHERIFF of a county the size of Lincoln, fifty years ago, was assuredly no sinecure. The duties were both arduous and extremely hazardous. Lincoln County included an area sufficient to form a state in itself; in fact, its area of nearly fifty thousand square miles was equal to the two states of Massachusetts and Connecticut combined. To travel from the county seat, Lincoln, to any of the other settlements, involved a journey of one or more days either on horseback or in a buckboard. Although the disorder which resulted from the Lincoln County War had been brought under control, officers of the law had plenty to do, and that, sometimes, at the risk of their own lives, in controlling the desperate characters still in the county.

John William Poe became sheriff in January, 1882, following Pat Garrett, who did not again become a candidate after his 1880-82 term. When the Democratic county convention met in the summer of 1881, John William was nominated sheriff, and, as Lincoln County was overwhelmingly Democratic, this assured his election a few months later.

There were in the county at this time thirteen precincts: Lincoln, San Patricio, Picacho, Seven Rivers, Los Tablos, Roswell, White Oaks, Peñasco, South Fork, Nogal, Bonito, and Gallinas.

One of John William's first moves, after becoming sheriff, was to pick his assistants for the enforcement of the laws. Jim Brent was chief deputy. J. Smith Lea, or "Cousin Smith," as he was more familiarly known, was made deputy and jailor. Smith had a host of friends and admirers and was a true pioneer in every sense of the word.

The fall term of court came in September, and it was a busy time for John William. The activity of the officers had filled the jail with prisoners awaiting trial, many of whom would undoubtedly be convicted. Then it would become the duty of John William and his assistants to see that the sentences were carried out. If, as was most generally the case, the judge sentenced a prisoner to a term in the penitentiary, it would be necessary to convey him to Leavenworth, Kansas, where the government penitentiary was located, for New Mexico was still without a penal institution.

The most important case on the docket that fall was that of Eddie House, under indictment for the murder of a Mexican sheepherder. He and his old father, both from New York State, were alleged to have plotted to kill the herders in charge of a large flock of sheep and to appropriate the animals to themselves. They had engaged a white man named Crow and a negro named Logwood to assist them. All four—hirelings and instigators—had been captured by John William and his deputies and lodged in jail at Lincoln.

Shortly before court convened, a cowboy named Pearl rode into Fort Stanton and, being pretty well "tanked up" on bad whisky, he engaged in a drunken brawl with some soldiers. The melee reached its height when Pearl drew his pistol and killed one of the soldiers. He was immediately arrested, taken to Lincoln, and placed in jail. As John William was in White Oaks that day, Smith Lea took charge of Pearl and locked him in the back compartment of the jail, where he was presumably well confined.

Two nights later, a group of soldiers from the fort came into Lincoln after midnight. They broke down the jail door, took Pearl out and hanged him to a tree. In their operations they moved so cautiously and silently that they did not even awaken the jailor. But they failed to fasten the jail door after taking Pearl out, and all the other prisoners escaped, Crow, House, and Logwood among them. Several of the prisoners—particularly those awaiting trial for minor offenses—returned the next day. They had concluded that it was better to get their trials over with than to be "on the dodge" as fugitives from justice. When they applied for reinstatement as prisoners, they explained their absence by saying they had merely been "taking a little constitutional in the sunlight."

When John William learned what had happened to his four most important prisoners, he hurried back to Lincoln to lead his deputies on a manhunt. He had been informed that House, Logwood, and Crow had been seen on the road to Nogal, evidently making for the Rio Grande. Taking Jim Brent and a deputy who lived at White Oaks, he followed the trail until they overtook the trio about sundown in a large flat near the Rio Grande. The fugitives were on foot and as soon as they saw the posse they scattered and took to the underbrush.

The posse captured House before dark, but were entirely unable to locate the other two, although they knew they could not be far away. The brush made a very safe place of concealment, and the posse had to content themselves with the single prisoner they had retaken.

The House case came to trial at the next term of court, and was bitterly contested. Mrs. House, the prisoner's mother, came out from New York and secured the best legal talent obtainable. Her presence in the courtroom during the trial created a wave of sympathy for her son. Her story was to the effect that her son had always been wayward, and had been influenced in such a way by her husband that his natural rascality had been deepened. At the end of ten days, the verdict was that Eddie House was not guilty. An acquittal was really almost a foregone conclusion, since there were no witnesses to the deed and the two accomplices were yet at large.

Just before midnight, on the day preceding the adjournment of court, there was a hammering on the door of the sheriff's office. Smith Lea, aroused from sleep, called out, "Who's there?" Upon opening the door, he found a frightened Mexican who had come to confess to a killing.

He stated that he had heard a noise like a large animal shuffling around his house and, supposing his chickens were in danger, he had snatched up his rifle and fired. When he investigated, he discovered that he had killed a neighbor who, too drunk to find his way home, had been crawling on all fours in the vicinity of the henhouse. As court was still in session it was possible to dispose of this case *"pronto."* The straightforward confession of the killer so impressed the jury that a verdict of justifiable homicide was rendered.

A few months later John William heard that the escaped negro Logwood was near Fort Union in the employ of a Captain Arrington, so he went after the escaped prisoner. He rode his big bay Dan the two hundred miles to Las Vegas and put his horse in a livery stable there. A man named Brown drove him out to the Arrington ranch. John William timed himself to arrive about dusk, so he could ask for entertainment for the night, and have time enough to quietly investigate the situation.

The next morning John William confided his errand to his host, but the latter felt there must be a mistake in thinking Logwood was the man in his employ. He admitted having a negro working for him, but scouted the idea that he was a criminal.

"Why," Captain Arrington said, "my wife and children are very much attached to this negro. He hasn't shown any criminal inclinations while he has been here. But, even though I believe you're mistaken, of course I won't interfere. You do what you consider is your duty in the matter."

"Well, Captain Arrington," John William replied, "I think I must take this man back to Lincoln with me. Will you call him in? Ask him to come here to the house on some pretext that won't rouse his suspicions."

Captain Arrington stepped outside and called to the negro, who was busy at some work in the yard.

"Go to the corral and bring the gentleman's rig up to the house."

When the buckboard arrived, John William stepped out of the house and from the corner of his eye took a good look at the negro. He felt instantly certain that it was Logwood, so he drew his pistol and pointed it.

"All right, Logwood!" he said grimly. "Climb in. You're going back to Lincoln with me. And don't cut any side steps, either."

"You's making a mistake, Mister Sheriff! My name ain't Logwood. It's Norwood," the prisoner protested.

"All *woods* look alike to me today," John William told him. "Put out your hands for the cuffs. I haven't any time to argue with you."

When he had handcuffed the negro and got him into the buckboard, John William ordered his driver to get back to Las Vegas as quickly as possible, and the liveryman whipped up the team. But on the way into town they overtook an itinerant preacher and gave him a lift.

The "reverend" climbed into the front seat with the driver, but kept turning to talk to John William, who guarded the prisoner in the back. While they were driving, a large hawk circled close overhead, and the preacher said:

"Can you hit that, Sheriff?"

John William jerked up his six-shooter and almost before the question was asked, it was answered. The negro stared at the dead hawk and shook his head slightly.

The preacher talked intermittently about that shot all the way to Vegas. And when he was thanking John William for the ride and saying goodbye, he looked at the negro:

"Don't you forget what happened to that hawk!" he said.

From Las Vegas southward sheriff and prisoner rode, the negro on a rented horse. The two hundred miles were covered in three days and during that time John William never relaxed his watch; he went sleepless until the prisoner was safe in Lincoln jail again. One of the prisoners asked the negro why he hadn't tried to escape, on the long road to Lincoln.

"Uh-uh!" he said. "Uh-uh. This nigger's no fool. That man never batted an eye all the time. And I seen him shoot *one* hawk on the wing!"

This time Logwood stayed in jail until his case came up for trial at the spring term of court. He admitted his identity and turned state's evidence. He pleaded guilty to the robbery, but claimed he didn't know whether or not he had killed anyone when he fired at the herders—which, he claimed, he was ordered to do by House. He received a sentence of ten years in the penitentiary.

But not always was the recapture of escaped prisoners accomplished so simply and easily by the sheriff and his deputies. One of the most desperate encounters he had in all his years as an officer was with an escaped convict named Nicolas Aragon. This was late in 1884, just as John William was beginning his second term as sheriff.

Aragon had been arrested and convicted of murder during the May term of court and sentenced to twenty-five years in the penitentiary. As soon as he was back in jail he told a fellow prisoner that he would die before he served that term. Some time later he asked Smith Lea, the jailor, to let him help cook. As he appeared to be an exemplary prisoner, the request was granted. It seemed impossible for any prisoner to escape over the sixteen-foot wall which enclosed the jail, especially when (as in the case of Aragon) he was kept ironed. But one night he sawed his shackles apart and scaled the high wall without being detected. His escape, made in September, 1884, brought an offer of two hundred dollars reward from Governor Sheldon.

In November it was reported that Aragon was hiding at Gallinas Springs, forty miles south of Las Vegas. John William dispatched one of his deputies, Joseph N. ("Dad") Corn, to capture the outlaw. "Dad" rode up to the hut in which Aragon was hiding, and hailed it. But before he had time to dismount Aragon shot him through the heart.

Again the desperado fled. He succeeded in keeping his hiding place a secret for a considerable time. The killing of Deputy Corn placed still another reward upon his head and redoubled the energy with which the hunt for him was carried on.

Information came to John William late in December concerning Aragon's whereabouts, and he prepared to go after the murderer himself. He knew very well the risk involved, so he took me as far as Roswell and left me with the Pierces so that, if the worst came, I would be with friends. Then he went back to Lincoln and took three of his most trusted deputies—Johnny Hurley, Jim Brent, and Barney Mason—on Aragon's trail.

In the meantime, as it was near Christmas, I was enjoying at Roswell some of the festivities of the holiday season. I had no suspicion that anything special was happening to my husband. The first inkling came while a *baile* was in progress at the Pierces'. I was moving through the intricate calls of a quadrille when I heard a sudden commotion at the door. A cowboy named Jim Gilchrist had stepped in excitedly without knocking and was moving toward me. His face indicated bad news.

Instantly the dance stopped. Others had also seen Jim's face. Captain Lea pushed quickly across the room, intercepting Gilchrist.

"What's up, Jim?" he asked in a low tone.

"I just rode in from Anton Chico, Captain," the cowboy answered excitedly. "Poe's up there with a posse. They got Aragon corralled in an old house. Been holding him there ever since Sunday afternoon. Johnny Hurley's been killed—shot through the body by Aragon. Jim Brent's got a hole through his hat—mighty close squeak, he had."

My head whirled, and I grew faint. Now I understood why John William had brought me down to Roswell! He had feared the outcome of this attempt to recapture Aragon. Then Jim Gilchrist added a few more details:

"Brent's gone to Las Vegas to bring Pat Garrett and some dynamite. The snow's a foot deep around the house. They've tried to fire it, but the roof's covered with snow, and it won't light."

Gilchrist's details gave me great relief. I could gather that John William had thus far not been injured, though if Brent had gone to Las Vegas, he was holding Aragon at bay with only Barney Mason to help. That meant the danger was far from being over.

When the mail buckboard arrived next morning, all of Roswell was at the post office to learn further news of the encounter. The driver reported that it had ended by the Mexican's finally surrendering. He had been taken to Las Vegas and lodged in jail there, suffering from a bad scalp wound, and another serious one in the leg. John William was alive and unhurt; likewise Jim Brent and Barney Mason, but poor Johnny Hurley was dead.

Two or three days later John William returned. He was tired and worn from exposure to the cold and from the intense nervous strain to which he had been subjected. I clung to him frantically, crying on his shoulder and begging him to give up his office as sheriff. John William petted me and promised that he would soon do as I wished.

"Now I know why you brought me down to Roswell," I told him. "You were afraid you might not come back."

John William nodded.

"I knew I was taking chances. Aragon is a desperate character, and I knew it wouldn't be easy to capture him. I had an idea it might be a case of kill or be killed for some of us. Poor Johnny got his the first thing. After that, the rest of us would have stayed there till hell froze over, rather than let that scoundrel escape."

He had taken as a posse Jim Brent, Johnny Hurley, Barney Mason, Billy Dufer, and Jim Abercrombie. About midnight they reached the house where Aragon was reported to be hiding. It was bitterly cold, and the posse, wading through a foot of snow, were half-frozen.

John William knocked on the door and waited. He could hear movement inside, but nobody answered the knock, so he called that Sheriff Poe was there with a warrant for Nicolas Aragon. A woman replied that Aragon was not there; only she and another woman were in the house.

John William told them to come outside, and when they had obeyed he sent them with Johnny Hurley, who spoke Spanish fluently, into a wing of the house built at right angles to that section from which they had come—and in which John William believed Aragon was hiding.

"Talk to them," John William ordered Hurley. "Try to find out where Aragon is, if he really isn't in there."

The rest of the posse scattered to guard the house. Shortly, Johnny Hurley came out of the wing where he had taken the women. He was excited and he came around the corner of the house and walked past the door of the main section.

"We've got him, all right!" he called. "He's in there!"

John William realized that Aragon could both hear and see Hurley and he yelled quickly:

"Johnny! Get away from that door—quick! He'll kill you!"

And Aragon fired through the door at that instant. Hurley staggered.

"I'm bad-hit!" he cried. "I'm gut-shot!"

He went back around the corner of the house and into the room where he had interviewed the women. There he lay in front of the fire, groaning, suffering terribly from a wound in the stomach. The posse did all possible to make him comfortable, but there was no medical help to be had, and he died in agony.

While Johnny Hurley was dying the shooting was general, both inside and outside. Every time a posseman exposed himself Aragon shot at him. John William had the closest escape from death that he had ever known, not excepting even the moment when he faced Billy the Kid at Sumner over the Kid's drawn pistol.

He had sheltered himself behind an adobe wall which fenced in the yard and was trying to locate Aragon through a window. Aragon saw him without being seen and fired from another window.

John William was ducking behind the wall when the shot came. The slug plowed through the top of the wall and knocked off John William's hat and filled his eyes with dust from the mud bricks. An inch higher, a second sooner, and the bullet would have caught him between the eyes.

When he told me of this narrow escape I begged him again to resign his office. But he shook his head.

"Somebody has to do this work. I feel that it's my job right now to help rid the country of these desperadoes and make the county a place for decent people to live safely. But I promise you I won't run for sheriff when my term's up."

He was not the only one of the posse to have a near escape. Jim Brent tried for a shot at Aragon through the window, and a bullet from the murderer tore off the rim of his hat. The posse fired into the door and through all the windows at every possible angle, trying to kill Aragon with a glancing bullet. But for sixty hours the battle went on, the posse exposed to the intense cold outdoors, without food. The strain told on them all, but Jim Brent was most affected.

He had developed neuralgia, and was suffering intensely. So when John William decided to send to Las Vegas for help, Brent was chosen as messenger. He could accomplish two things at once—get medical attention for himself, and send help. He was to try to find Pat Garrett, but if he couldn't find Garrett, the sheriff of San Miguel County was to be asked to send assistance.

John William gave all praise to Jim Brent for making the trip successfully when all the odds were against him. On his way to Vegas, he came to a creek that was frozen over. His horse refused to cross it, and Jim could get the animal ahead only by himself dismounting and breaking the ice and wading through, leading the horse. When he reached Vegas, both his feet were frozen. Garrett was somewhere over in the Panhandle. But the Mexican sheriff was an energetic officer. The next morning, nervy Jim Brent came back with him and his reënforcements. The Mexican officer held a parley with Aragon, and the desperado agreed to surrender if he were promised protection. The promise was given, and he came out with his hands up.

The officers admitted that Aragon had made a remarkable fight. When he finally surrendered, he had been wounded three times in the course of battle. One shot had cut a furrow through his heavy hair, just grazing the scalp above the forehead. Another had struck him in a corner of the forehead and plowed through the skin for three or four inches before turning away from the skull. Those two wounds alone must have given him a glimpse of Eternity for a few seconds! But the wound that had been mostly responsible for disabling him and forcing him to surrender was a vicious hole through the calf of one of his legs. This gave him a great deal of pain and, while not a dangerous wound, it broke his fighting spirit. The posse came off without a scratch, save in the case of poor Johnny Hurley.

Aragon was kept securely confined in the Las Vegas jail until his trial. He was first tried for the killing of "Dad" Corn, but was acquitted under the defense that he did not know Corn was an officer and that Corn had fired first. He was next tried for the killing of Johnny Hurley and had no defense to offer in this case. He was sentenced to the penitentiary for life but after serving ten years of this sentence, he was pardoned. He returned to his old neighborhood, where he died a natural death some years later.

He had "distinguished" himself in one of the longest and hardest-fought battles between desperadoes and officers of the law in all the records of New Mexico.

As John William was almost ill from exposure and nervous strain, we started for home next day—we were living on the VV Ranch then—stopping in Lincoln long enough for him to see Mrs. Hurley and condole with her over the killing of her husband. She was a Mexican woman of fine character.

On the VV, my sister Edith and I soon fell back into the usual routine of ranch life, riding our horses out over the range or making calls on our partner's family and Mrs. Garrett. My brother Fred had come back to be with us at night. John William continued to pay us week-end visits as he came and went on his arduous work as an officer.

It was during one of these flying week-end visits, and some weeks after the fight with Aragon, that we saw Jim Brent come dashing around the bend of the big hill, spurring as though his life depended on reaching the ranch as quickly as possible.

"A bad killing over on the Block Ranch!" he yelled to John William, who had hurried to the gate to meet him.

"Can you wait until I get a fresh horse? Old Dan's pretty well tuckered out."

"There's plenty of time," Brent said. "The fellows who did the killing have given themselves up. But we'll have to go over and recover the bodies."

Then Brent told us quickly what had happened.

A man named Richards, with a partner, had taken up a claim above the Block Ranch, fifteen miles from Fort Stanton. The Bennett brothers, who had also taken up a claim, were said to have suffered a great deal of injury from Richards and his partner. The two had destroyed a foundation the Bennetts had just completed for their cabin home, and had warned the Bennetts to leave the place for good, under a penalty which they did not name, but which was evident enough.

Next, the Bennetts found the water that ran through their claim diverted around by Richards' place. So they took their guns and started for the head of the stream. In the underbrush on the mountain side a battle began. Richards and his men were in hiding. It was certain, according to Jim Brent, that the Richards side began the fight, but they did not live to finish it. The Bennetts killed Richards and his partner, then came in and gave themselves up.

This was more or less the usual sort of incident with which John William dealt in his capacity as a peace officer.

The tragedy at the Mayberry home was perhaps the most bloody and ghastly in all the annals of the sheriff's office during John William's term. He did not have to make any arrests in connection with this case, for the distracted man who "ran amuck" and slaughtered nine persons came to his death at the hands of others, who had hurried to the scene and instituted a search for the murderer.

John William, at that time, had been in White Oaks for several days. Little Johnny Mayberry, who was a frequent visitor at our ranch home, had been with us for several hours one evening. He went home at nine o'clock.

About three o'clock the following morning, I was awakened by a man outside calling for the sheriff.

"He's over at White Oaks," I replied, and then inquired, "What's the matter?"

"There's a terrible killing going on, up on the Bonito," the man told me. "We want the sheriff right away."

"Take a fresh horse from the stable and ride to White Oaks for him," I suggested.

But the man replied:

"I can't take the time; I'm going back to Bonito."

He whirled his horse and thundered away.

Early that morning Jim Brent came over to the ranch, his horse worn out from hard riding, to see John William.

"He's at White Oaks, Mr. Brent," I replied, "but you ought to go over to the Bonito. Something terrible has happened over there. Some man called here at three o'clock this morning for Mr. Poe. Take a horse and get over there as fast as you can make it."

I had hardly finished speaking before Brent was stripping the saddle from his own mount and throwing it on John William's big bay, which happened to be there. I waited in great suspense all the long day for further news of what had occurred up on the Rio Bonito, but it was not until nightfall that I learned the details.

John William was notified at White Oaks, and he and Brent made a mad ride for Bonito. They came home exhausted, their faces showing that they had been through some terrible experience. As I served them the strong coffee I had ready, Jim Brent said:

"I went through the Civil War, but I never saw such a sight as the one at the Mayberrys'."

He went on to say that a man named Martin Nelson, who was living with the Mayberrys and who, up to the night before, had been considered a peaceable man, suddenly went crazy. He seemed to be bent on wiping out the whole family. It was supposed that he first killed a Dr. Flynn, of Cincinnati, a boarder at the Mayberrys'. Possibly there had been bad feeling between the two.

His next victim was little Johnny Mayberry, who, seemingly hearing the shot that killed Dr. Flynn, rushed into the room to see what was going on. Nelson had then apparently gone into the next room and killed four-year-old Eddie Mayberry. Mr. Mayberry doubtless had been roused and had rushed upstairs. It was thought that he had been killed next.

Mrs. Mayberry started up the stairs, but Nelson shot her as she appeared. She was not killed instantly, for she had run downstairs and out of the house, falling into an irrigation ditch. There her body had been found.

Pete Nelson, who kept a saloon near by, heard the firing at the Mayberry place and ran over. He, too, was shot down by Martin Nelson. Another man, whose name nobody seemed to know, was looking in at the back window of the saloon, hoping to see Martin Nelson, who he thought had taken refuge there. He was seen by the murderer and shot in the back. Nelly Mayberry was also shot, but not fatally.

Nelson ran short of ammunition, and apparently decided to get something to eat. He went up the cañon to the house of an old German named Deidrich and forced the woman there to make coffee for him. Then he returned to the scene of his wholesale slaughter, to be shot and killed by Rudolph Schultz and Don Campbell, who were watching for him.

Jim Brent remarked that the two men saved the county the trouble and expense of capturing

Nelson and trying him, although if the officers had captured him they must have had to surrender him to citizens bent on miners' justice.

Our acquaintance with the Mayberrys made this tragedy the more terrible to us. I had asked little Johnny Mayberry to stay the night with us. But he had gone home to meet his death a few hours later.

A few months later John William had his last encounter with desperadoes. And he stood face to face with death as he had done on two previous instances—the midnight meeting with Billy the Kid, in July of 1881, and the long-drawn battle with Nicolas Aragon, in December of 1884.

Over on the Peñasco two desperate characters, Sutton and Nixon, were hiding in the woods. They had murdered a ranchman in a row over land rights, and the sheriff's office had warrants for their arrests. Accompanied by Jim Brent, John William departed to "get" the murderers. Nixon was captured without much trouble, while he was making his morning coffee in a deserted cabin. After handcuffing him and hobbling his ankles, the sheriff and his deputy left their prisoner in the house and went to look around for Sutton, who was regarded as the more desperate of the two.

Many years after, I heard from Jim Brent (then an old man living in Silver City, New Mexico) the details of the close call which John William had at that time.

"The only reason why Poe wasn't shot and killed there was because of his great nerve. We were in the timber, and just as Poe was about to pass a big pine tree, a gun was stuck in his face, and Sutton cried:

" 'Stick 'em up! Don't you move, or I'll pump you full of lead!'

"Poe never flinched. He kept his eyes right on Sutton and walked right to the muzzle of his gun. He said:

" 'You don't want to shoot me, Sutton. I'm an officer of the law and to kill me means death to you sooner or later. I'm only doing my duty. I've got a warrant for your arrest.'

"All the time Poe was talking he kept his eyes steady on Sutton, and I reckon he must have hypnotized the fellow, like a snake charms a bird. Anyhow, Sutton surprised us both by putting down his gun and submitting to being handcuffed without a word. I never saw the like in all my experience with outlaws and desperadoes. All that saved Poe was his cool, deliberate nerve."

John William's promise to me to end his career as a peace officer with the expiration of his second term was fulfilled sooner than either of us anticipated. He was always quick to push forward into new opportunities. He had proved this in his boyish ambition to get into the West; it had also shown itself in his buffalo-hunting days, when he was called an "outside hunter," a man who always located his camps farther out than any of his competitors. The characteristic had cropped out, too, when he settled in Lincoln County, then probably as remote and inaccessible and lawless as any section of the United States.

Now, it was South America. He and his close friend, Smith Lea, had become interested in reading about opportunities awaiting men who could face new conditions and open up extensive cattle ranches down in the Argentine Republic. Although cattle and ranch properties were booming in the States, yet these two men, with the spirit and temper of the frontiersman, decided upon the Argentine as offering what they most desired, which, after all, was "a new field to conquer."

When he decided to leave for South America on a trip of investigation, John William tendered his resignation to the Governor. Accompanying his letter was another, recommending that Jim Brent be appointed sheriff for the rest of John William's term. There was no doubt that Brent was the man for the place, and when the news came that the Governor had adopted the suggestion, and made Brent the new sheriff, everyone was delighted.

At Lincoln, Brent was given a great *baile* for send-off. Everybody was there, from near and far, filling the hall to its utmost capacity. The Montaña boys furnished the music with violin and guitar. Personally, I was irritated because of some gossip I had heard, and refused to accompany John William. That was "cutting off my nose to spite my face," for the *baile* proved to be the most enjoyable affair that Lincoln had ever put on.

Even John William "celebrated," for he broke two rigid rules of his life—never to dance, never to drink to excess. On this particular night he did both. The revelry grew in volume, and Jimmie Dolan and Josh Church proposed to make it an unforgettable occasion; so they proceeded to mix the drinks. Everyone was soon hilariously "full." Even John William—so it was reported to me—dancing with Doña Baca, "swung corners" like a dancing master.

When Eugenio Salazar cried: "All promenade to your seats!" Doña Baca remarked to Mrs. Cockrell: "Mr. Poe is very much the gentleman, but he *is* just a little drunk!"

As a natural result of the celebration, every man in attendance was suffering with *"delorde cabeza"*—swelled head—next morning.

But they all felt that the occasion was worth the effort. Brent made a fine sheriff and left a splendid record behind him.

Fortune Favors the Ex-Sheriff

WHEN JOHN WILLIAM turned over the sheriff's office to his successor, Jim Brent, he informed me that the first matter on the program was our long-delayed honeymoon trip.

For myself, I had no desire whatever to travel west at that moment. The Apaches on the San Carlos Reservation in Arizona were causing much trouble that winter. I was desperately afraid of the Indians. Stories of their depredations came regularly to us. At one ranch a woman and young daughter were killed. Their mutilated bodies had been discovered hanging from hooks on the back wall of their cabin.

But John William persuaded me that it was safe to travel. And our railroad facilities had been increased. The Rock Island had pushed its line from the northeast corner of New Mexico toward the southwest. Socorro was now our nearest point, instead of Las Vegas where I had arrived three years before. Not that it was much an improvement in distance, for even Socorro was almost two hundred miles from Lincoln. However, by driving early and late and having several changes of teams, the new stage line made the trip in two days and a night.

So we started one morning toward Socorro. My uneasiness was lightened a little when I saw

Mr. Ozane, owner of the line, climb up beside the driver, for that meant another able-bodied man to fight, if we happened to be attacked by the Apaches.

Our route took us out of the mountains by the steep Nogal Hill. We skirted the rough *malpais*— bad country—lying in the Tularosa Basin, then crossed the next range of mountains and descended into the Rio Grande Valley.

As we turned north into the valley, our route coincided with the upper part of the famous Jornado del Muerto, the "Journey of Death" of the Spanish explorers, so named because of its formidable distance of ninety miles without a watering place.

The stage journey was made without real dangers, though I was nervous all the time. Once I thought my fears were to be completely justified. It was about eleven o'clock of the second night out when I heard Ozane shouting to the driver to stop. I *knew* that the savages were on us. And John William had jumped off almost as soon as Ozane's yell sounded. I screamed to him:

"Take me off! Help me out of here! Don't let me be massacred in this old stage!"

But it was only a small matter on a Southwestern stage line. One of the horses had slipped into a gully, and as soon as he could be got out and put back into harness, we went on. I was very quiet for awhile, thoroughly ashamed of my fright.

Our destination was Hot Springs, Arkansas, then one of the liveliest cities of the country. Health baths and horse races seemed to be the principal occupations of the visitors. We were in Hot Springs for several weeks and found it crowded with visitors from every walk of life, every conceivable locality. Noticeable, particularly, were the gamblers with their checked suits and diamond studs.

But the most fascinating part of Hot Springs was the beautiful horses at the track. They were so alive to the contests they figured in, so intent—it seemed—on winning the races. I suppose my early days on a California stock farm had bred in me a love for fine horses which could never be dimmed.

On our way home to New Mexico we stopped for a few days in Missouri with John William's parents, Nathan and Louisa Poe, who had moved there from Kentucky. Then, because John William had a new urge—this time to settle in South America—we hurried back to Roswell.

In January of 1887, John William and Smith Lea went down to Argentina to look for a location on which they might establish a large cattle ranch. They reached Buenos Aires in February and for several days looked over the beautiful parks and monuments and boulevards of the capital.

Their search for a ranch then carried them across the vast *pampas* by rail almost due west to Mendoza. They were enthusiastic about these immense plains with the great herds of cattle and horses and sheep. The country seemed a ranchman's paradise. Before they reached Mendoza they saw the vineyards stretching away for miles and miles across the plains, burdened with the grapes which made *Mendoza Port* famous, even then, the world over.

From Mendoza they rode seventy miles toward the Andes. At last a location was discovered which promised ideal conditions for a ranch. There was grass and water, and the price was twenty-five cents an acre—as contrasted to the two hundred and fifty dollars an acre now asked for that same land!

No purchase was made at that time. John William saw the necessity for improvements. Too, he must return to the United States to bring me down. So the partners turned back toward the Rio de la Plata. They went by rail to Rosario, then made a voyage up the Paraná, a noble river having its source far up toward the mouth of the Amazon. Their voyage took them as far as Corrientes, a town situated at the juncture of the Paraná and Philcomayo rivers, in the southwestern corner of Paraguay. They ascended the Philcomayo as far as Asunción.

Paraguay at that time was as primitive as the Garden of Eden. It was then, even more than now, "a land of women," for the men had been almost exterminated in a series of wars with Brazil, Bolivia, Uruguay, and the Argentine Republic. Polygamy was the natural result of these conditions. I recall a letter from the travelers containing the statement that there were thirteen women to one man, and Smith Lea's addition that the women's only clothing was a finger ring and a smile.

Paraguayans they found a simple, friendly folk, and the land was so fertile that a rich harvest was had by merely scraping the top of the ground and sowing the seed.

Coming back, they stopped for sight-seeing—more or less involuntarily, for the single line of steamships operating between New York and Buenos Aires was owned and operated by the Arbuckle-Thurber Coffee Company. The firm was satisfied to have its vessels make one journey in either direction in a month. So passengers had good long looks at Rio de Janeiro and Bahia and other ports.

Back in the States, Smith Lea stopped in Tennessee to visit his mother, whom he had not seen for several years. So John William came back to New Mexico alone, arriving in midsummer. I remember that it was on the first day of August that I drove the buckboard from Lincoln to Fort Stanton to meet him.

He had a great deal to say about South America. But after much thought he decided against leaving his native country. New Mexico, he believed, offered plenty of opportunity for a man seeking his fortune. And for him, who had become identified with the territory and was well and favorably known over it, it should not be hard to attain success. And this was a decision he never regretted.

As first step in his campaign, he bought a tract of land five miles southeast of Roswell. There were plenty to laugh when he announced his intention of bringing new thought and modern methods into the cattle business. But he went calmly about his experiment of raising cattle "under fence"—something that not even John Chisum, "high priest" of the section as regards cattle, had ever attempted.

John William sowed his land to alfalfa, bordering each forty-acre field with a row of cottonwoods to give shade for his stock. He stocked the ranch with three hundred and fifty highbred cattle and a hundred and fifty brood mares of equal quality. For he planned to raise mules as well as cattle. This was the first stock farm, in the modern sense of the term, in eastern New Mexico, if not in the entire territory.

Alfalfa proved a highly profitable crop, and John William's experiment opened the way to what has become the leading feature of development in the Pecos Valley. The yield of John William's fields was amazing. Four tons to the acre and four cuttings a season was the average crop. At the prevailing price of ten dollars a ton, it was easy to compute the profits!

The Poe alfalfa stacks became famous in the neighborhood. A local wag said one day, as he passed our place with a friend:

"What's that mountain over there?"

The other man stared, then answered seriously:

"That's not a mountain. It's one of John Poe's alfalfa stacks."

"Well, well!" the joker said—just as solemnly. "I thought he had moved Capitán Mountain down into his field."

At the same time that he was developing his stock farm, John William made a business connection in Roswell that grew stronger with the years.

He was for a long time in partnership with Smith
Lea and William H. Cosgrove in the mercantile
business. He bought the original store, then owned
by Captain Lea and C. B. Bonney, an adobe building situated on what today is the northwest corner
of Main and Fourth Streets, in Roswell. The new
firm did business under the name of Poe, Lea &
Cosgrove. But after some years John William and
Smith Lea sold their interests to Cosgrove. Later,
John William acquired the land on which the old
store building had stood for so long. He built on
the site, in 1905, a group of stores called, appropriately enough, "The Pioneer Block."

He loved the land and was never so happy as
when he stood among growing things. His great
fields of purple-blooming alfalfa, shoulder-high to
us as we walked through it; his calves and mule
colts galloping and playing; even the hard-working
beaver which often played havoc with the irrigating system—all these interested and amused John
William.

Near Roswell our ranch lay under the Pumpkin
Row Ditch—named for the famous pumpkins
which were grown along it. The ditch was fed by
the water from South Spring River, and John William made its banks solid by planting Bermuda
grass along them. Often, he shouldered a spade
and walked the length of the irrigating ditch,
watching for any break or, very frequently, merely
to look over a beaver dam.

Again and again he found the *acequia* as dry as

a bone. And Louis, the hired man, would shake his head and say:

"Must be the beaver again!"

Riding his horse Dixie up to the head of the canal one day, he was astonished to find a great cottonwood tree dropped across the ditch for foundation of a big dam.

The war was unceasing between farmer and beaver. When two of the hands decided to solve the problem with a scarecrow, they underestimated the opposition.

"If we take one of Mr. Poe's old suits," they said, "and rig it up on some sticks, the beaver will think they have got human beings to deal with and they'll be scared off."

But within a few days the scarecrow disappeared, and when it was found, coat, hat, and pants were almost buried in the mud, as if the beaver had "massacred" it. Then all the hands turned to on "Deep Pool" and turned it back into the river, forcing the beaver to find a new home.

For nine busy, interesting years, John William and I lived on the ranch. Then, one day, he came home to announce that he had sold the place to J. J. Hagerman, a railroad magnate of Colorado Springs who had become interested in eastern New Mexico and wanted to make his home in the vicinity of Roswell.

"Well, then, what are you going to do next?" I asked.

"I think I'll try banking," he said.

So he became associated with E. A. Cahoon in the *Bank of Roswell*, which was just then beginning a remarkable history as the commercial mainstay of the Pecos Valley for more than forty years.

When the bank opened in 1890 it was the only institution of the kind within a radius of two hundred and twenty-five miles.

In 1893, John William was elected president of the bank. He held this position until he decided to dispose of his stock. In 1899 the bank aspired to become a "national," and in the reorganization that followed, which gave it the present name of *First National Bank*, John William retired.

In 1894 he had erected a bank building and this he sold at the time of his retirement. The building was later razed to make room for the beautiful structure which now occupies the site at the corner of Main and Third Streets.

In October of 1895, John William made good a promise of years before. We moved into that new home which he had promised me under the shadow of Sierra Blanca on the day that I walked into the tiny log cabin of our first ranch.

This new house was a story-and-a-half cottage built on an entire half block, on the northeast corner of Seventh and Kentucky Streets. It was soon called Roswell's most beautiful home, because of its overshadowing trees, its vine-clad walls and fine old rose gardens filled with rare plants.

At this time Roswell was becoming a town of considerable importance. It had been slow in passing the infant stage, but was then growing lustily. J. J. Hagerman had given it railroad connection with the outside world by building what was originally called The Pecos Valley & Southeastern Railroad. This line extended to Pecos City, Texas, and became an inlet for many new settlers up and down the Pecos Valley. Mr. Hagerman identified himself with the valley and personally did a great deal to promote its development.

Hagerman bought many ranches around Roswell, notably the old Chisum headquarters ranch at South Spring River. There Mr. Hagerman replaced the rambling adobe house built by John Chisum— which I had visited when it was the outstanding house of the vicinity—with a twenty-room residence of brick. This was the Hagerman home.

Also, Hagerman constructed a large irrigating canal to carry water from North Spring River to the town of Hagerman twenty-five miles south of Roswell.

John William had given the Hagerman interests much of his attention while we lived on the stock farm. For several years he acted as a sort of local manager for all the pastures, canals, farms, orchards, and livestock belonging to Hagerman. But in 1894 his own interests became so many that he was forced to resign. Captain Jason W. James succeeded him.

John William was not long "out of harness" after retiring from the *First National Bank*. When in 1900 he announced his plan to organize a bank, applications for stock poured in. If the capital had been set at double the fifty thousand dollars he announced, still it would have been oversubscribed.

The new bank was named the *Citizens' Bank of Roswell*. John William was president, John Shaw, vice president, and Nathan Jaffa, cashier. In 1921 the bank absorbed the *American National Bank* of Roswell and became the *Citizens' National Bank*. John William continued as president.

It seems a far cry from buffalo hunting to banking. But actually the line of progress had been straightforward and firmly grounded. In the very beginning of his adult life, John William Poe had known what he wanted—to travel and to build a fortune. There were other considerations, of course; he was a particular sort of man with very definite characteristics. So in his climb upward, every move was made in accordance with his philosophy of life.

He worked on the railroad construction crew; he ranched with John Jacobs; he went out on the buffalo range; he served as an officer and as a stock detective and helped rid the Southwest of that little desperado, Billy the Kid—all in a sort of natural sequence of efforts to amass a fortune and at the same time do his share as a good citizen in civilizing the land which he had made his home.

Looking back now, on the near half century of his life in the Southwest, it all seems so simple! One of his enterprises leads so naturally to the next, and in each of them I see him the same John William Poe, forthright and strong-willed, developing rather than changing.

He was a pioneer and a frontiersman, but he kept abreast of progress. When he saw public work to be done, he came forward to perform his share of it. Occasionally there was a nominal wage for an office he held. Much more often there could be no pay except the satisfaction of aiding New Mexico.

In 1889 and 1890 he was appointed by Governor Miguel A. Otero to the Territorial Board of Equalization, when that board worked to distribute taxation equitably. When the New Mexico Military Institute was founded at Roswell in 1890, he became a member of the Board of Regents and continued as a member during the remainder of his life. At the time of his death he was treasurer.

From 1915 to 1917, after the admission of New Mexico to statehood had complicated the matter of taxation, he served as president of the State Tax Commission.

During the World War he accepted appointment as Fuel Administrator for New Mexico, despite the heavy pressure of his own business. And those who knew him intimately realized that his private affairs never received the close and conscientious attention that he gave to public business.

Neither of us ever developed completely the stay-at-home habit. When business permitted, John William was always anxious for an excursion. Sometimes we could go no more than a few miles from Roswell, to meet friends and go picnicking. But on other occasions we roamed with a longer tether. In 1907 we toured Ireland, England, the Netherlands, France, Italy, Austria, Germany, and Switzerland.

There was a long journey through Mexico and a leisurely trip by easy stages around the world in 1913. John William delighted in traveling through foreign countries and contrasting methods of life abroad with those seen in America.

He was strongly devoted to Masonry, having been made a Mason at Fort Griffin, Texas, the first initiate after founding of that lodge. And for forty years he worked in the order, being a charter member of the Roswell lodge, and among the first to receive the Commandery Degree in Roswell. Later he received the honorary Thirty-third Degree of the Scottish Rite.

He lived to see the wild Pecos Valley a garden spot, thickly settled where he had ridden his horse over fenceless mountain and plain. His end came quietly in July, 1923, and his real monument stands, not in South Park Cemetery, but in the broad alfalfa fields and orchards and homes for which he and his fellow pioneers cleared the way. His epitaph might be a sentence spoken of him by a friend:

"John Poe was one who never failed us."

Notes

Buffalo Hunting Is Profitable

JOE MCCOMBS was one of the historic figures around Fort Griffin. Edgar Rye uses him in *Quirt and Spur*, a book that gives a lifelike impression of old Fort Griffin, as an illustration of the lingual vagaries of the buffalo range. Since Joe McCombs was a law unto himself in regard to language, a prerogative he claimed in connection with his role of general funmaker, he perhaps is not an altogether fair example of the colloquiality of the range. Nevertheless, I am inclined to give Edgar Rye's account, both for what it may show about the lingo of the buffalo hunter, and about Joe himself:

The arrival of a buffalo hunter named Joe McCombs, from the camp of Poe and Jacobs, far out on the Western range, brought forth a series of questions and answers.

"Hello, Joe, give us your flipper, old man! Here, take a nip to cut the dust out of yer throat. Whar's yer bronco?"

"Petered out near Phantom Hill, and I hobbled him and had to huff it in."

"How are the boys in camp?"

"Oh, so-so, on an average—plenty of chuck, but no ammunition."

"Any trouble with the renegades and Indians?"

"Nope, not much. Little flurry last month when a bunch of the reds broke off the reservation corral near Fort Sill and came cavortin' down into the Panhandle. Dropped a few lead pills into our camp one evenin', and tried to stampede the ponies, but Poe turned loose his .45 and they skedaddled over the sand hills. Then a lieutenant with a bunch of buffalo soldiers rounded them up and drove them back to the reservation."

"Good season, Joe?"

"Sorter—nothing extry; buffalo gittin' skittish; hard to git a stand on 'em now."

"Where is your outfit, now?"

"Over the divide on the Deep Creek of the Colorado, not fur from Chisholm's Hole on the slant of the mesa. Dandy place; plenty of grass and water; oodles of turkeys and deer."

"Herds drifting?"

"Yep, grazin' north along the brakes, but kinder shy."

"When will you return?"

"Soon as some outfit gives me a lift back to Phantom, where I can ketch onto the bronco again."

"Well, drop in for your chuck, and we'll furnish you with a layout of blankets while you're in town."

"*Muchas gracias, señor;* I'll sure bunk down with you."

"All right, Joe; come and go when you please, old man, and no questions asked."

"You fellers are sure soshable; and if you ever hit the range, there will be a welcome waitin' for you."

Apprentice Peace Officer

FAMOUS IN THE SOUTHWEST was the "Lassiter Case" which had its origin in and around Fort Griffin. Since John William Poe was concerned with the affair only incidentally, it has been omitted from the narrative of his experiences while an officer of the town. But it seems to deserve recording because of the unusual motives and incidents involved, and for the length of time occupied in solving the mystery.

John Brock originally was a clerk in the post trader's store on the military reservation at Fort Griffin. He saw opportunity to start a ranch and so gave up his position to homestead a claim on Foyle Creek, some six miles west of the post.

With an old negro, Nick Williams, he built a log cabin and made the improvements necessary to comply with the homesteading laws.

The ranch prospered, and from time to time Brock increased his herd, which was marked with the GAB brand. He was ambitious, and the thought came to him that Ohio cattle would improve the quality of his stock. So he wrote to a cousin, Frank Lassiter, who lived at Oberlin, Ohio. He ordered a dozen shorthorn Durham cows and two registered bulls.

To insure good care of the cattle en route, he asked Lassiter to come to Texas with the shipment. Lassiter was to travel by train with the Durhams to Fort Worth—then the terminus of the railway —and to continue to Fort Griffin by easy stages over the trail.

Brock sent the negro, Williams, to meet his cousin. Williams drove a wagon that carried the camp outfit.

Lassiter made the drive without event, and when he arrived at the GAB on Foyle Creek, Brock offered him a half-interest in the property. Lassiter accepted, and the two men worked smoothly together until spring roundup started.

There were only a few of the GAB cattle on the range, so the partners decided that Lassiter alone could "rep," or serve as representative of their brand, at the general roundup. He started out with his outfit on a pack horse and rode with the other reps as the roundup wagons of many ranches shifted from one ground to another.

One morning Lassiter struck out across the prairie alone in the direction of Phantom Hill, to attend a gathering of cattle at the Mode Johnson ranch. Nothing more was seen of him—for fifteen years. The next evening his pack horse was discovered grazing on the GAB home ranch, but there was no other trace of Lassiter or his saddle horse. For several days a searching party headed by Brock scoured the plains, looking for traces of the missing man. But the search was fruitless; Lassiter had vanished as completely as though into thin air.

Suspicion fell heavily upon Brock. There were plenty to accuse him and the negro, Nick Williams, of having murdered Lassiter to secure the entire property for Brock. As the weeks passed and nothing was heard of Lassiter, suspicion became intensified to the point where the Vigilance Committee took cognizance of it. Hotheads were determined to summarily hang both Brock and the negro. But the conservative vigilantes suggested postponing the "necktie party" until the *corpus delicti* could be established, either by finding Lassiter's remains, or uncovering definite evidence of foul play.

Meanwhile, both Brock and Nick Williams were held in jail. In a short time, Frank Lassiter's brother Ed, with his wife, came out from Ohio. They took possession of the Brock ranch and did all they could to aid in fastening the guilt upon Brock. This crowd seemed determined to secure evidence, even going so far as to take the negro from the guard one night and swing him up to a tree in an effort to extort a confession from him that would implicate Brock. But Williams refused to confess any plot against Lassiter.

Brock knew that a formidable effort was being made to convict him and communicated with his father, who secured the services of an eminent attorney. The lawyer came out to Albany accompanied by Brock's brother. Through their efforts Brock and the negro were released on bonds of five thousand dollars and three thousand dollars respectively.

No sooner was Brock released than he became convinced that back of the whole affair was an attempt on the part of the Lassiters—Ed and Will, as well as Frank—to swindle him out of his property. He vowed he would expose the conspiracy and thereby vindicate himself. He employed a detective and started a systematic search for Frank Lassiter, whom he believed to be in hiding somewhere.

For fifteen years the search went on. When Brock had exhausted what money he might have in paying detectives for broadcasting photographs and other evidence, he would work awhile and save his wages until he had sufficient funds to continue the long search for the missing man.

The grand jury had failed to find an indictment, and this had exonerated Brock; but he was determined not to rest until he had received what he considered complete vindication. He became so obsessed with the idea of finding Lassiter, that people considered him "cracked" on the subject. He would talk of nothing else but the search for Lassiter. He traveled to Arizona, to New Mexico, and finally to Arkansas. For he had received a "tip" that a man living at Bentonville, Arkansas, seemed to answer the description of Frank Lassiter which had been broadcast.

When Brock arrived at Bentonville with a detective, he learned that the man who was suspected of being the vanished Lassiter had been living there for some three years; that he used the name of Laycock and had established himself in the community as a reputable citizen, for he had married a widow who owned the local pottery and managed the business for her.

When Brock confronted "Laycock" he recognized him instantly as the man he had hunted for so many years. But he was met by a flat denial from the suspected man.

"All right, then!" Brock said grimly. "If you're not Lassiter you won't have an L-shaped scar on your forehead. Lift his hat!" he demanded of the detective beside him.

The detective jerked off "Laycock's" hat and exposed the telltale scar.

"You're going back to Ohio, under arrest," Brock informed Lassiter. "They will recognize you in Oberlin, just as I did, in spite of that full beard you're wearing. And after all these years, you'll pay for the suspicion you threw on me, and the scheme you made to rob me of the GAB property. You didn't show any gratitude for my gift to you of half the outfit, and you didn't care that we were cousins. Neither do I, now! All I'm interested in is making you pay!"

When they were on the train, Brock continued to pour out all the stored-up bitterness of his ruined years. And Lassiter at last broke under the strain.

"I give up!" he told his cousin. "There's no use pretending any longer. For as soon as we come to Oberlin I'll be identified. So I'll tell you just what happened. You can believe it or not. It's a strange tale, but it *is* true."

Brock watched him suspiciously.

"When I started for Johnson's place," Lassiter said slowly, "I had no idea whatever of going away. But as I rode down that rocky trail that leads into Salt Creek Valley, my horse stumbled. I was thrown over his head and that's the last I remember until just the other day. You see, I was knocked senseless. When I came to, I was still dazed. I didn't know who I was or where I was.

"I managed to crawl to my horse and get on him somehow. He started away, and I was too weak and shaky even to try to guide him. You remember we bought that horse from a cowboy who had got him down at Vinita in the Indian Territory. Well, he started home, back toward Vinita. We made the Territory finally, and still I didn't know my name. At McAllister I went to work in the coal mines, and the other miners called me Laycock, because I looked like a man of that name who had been killed just before I got there."

"And you never did recover enough to know that you really were Lassiter, and that you'd come from Foyle Creek?" Brock demanded incredulously. "Not until just now?"

"Well, I was in pretty bad condition. I hardly remember where I wandered after I left the mines, or what I did before I got to Bentonville. Then my mind began to get a little clearer; I could work. I learned the pottery business and was very successful in it. Then I saw my picture in a newspaper with a story about Frank Lassiter. I thought maybe I was Frank Lassiter, but I didn't know why you wanted me; I couldn't guess what I might have done. I was afraid to inquire. And that's my story and it's every word absolute truth."

Lassiter seemed so entirely sincere that Brock could not help being impressed. He said that he accepted the account as truth. But he insisted that Lassiter must go on to Oberlin.

"Of course," Lassiter agreed. "It's only justice that I make up in every way possible for what you've suffered. If I had owned the courage I would have written you as soon as I saw that newspaper, to ask why you were hunting me."

He swore to Brock that he had never communicated with his brothers in all those years. If any underhand scheme had been afoot, engineered by Ed Lassiter, to get possession of the GAB Ranch, he knew nothing of it. He showed surprise when Brock told him that Ed Lassiter had been dead for several years.

In Oberlin, Frank Lassiter was identified by his former friends and his relatives. So Brock was vindicated at last. Lassiter deeded to him his interest in the homestead on Foyle Creek, then returned to Bentonville and his wife and pottery business.

Brock went back to Texas, carrying Lassiter's signed confession. All his friends congratulated him on the dogged search he had made and its successful climax. But those fifteen years of strain had exhausted him physically and mentally and financially. He lived only a few years.

When John William Poe encountered Brock some years afterward, in El Paso, Texas, and heard the long story of the hunt for Lassiter, the beginning of which he had known at firsthand in Fort Griffin, Brock was only the shadow of a man, prematurely aged, broken.

Trailing "Billy the Kid"

SIXTY-FIVE MILES northwest of Roswell lies the prehistoric city locally called Grand Quivira. Remains of ancient aqueducts and reservoirs confirm the belief that Grand Quivira at one time supported a population of several thousand. However, at the present time there is no water within a radius of fifty miles.

The consensus of opinion among archaeologists is that the city and the water supply were destroyed centuries ago by a stupendous upheaval of the earth. Beginning at the foot of the elevation once occupied by this city, a stream of molten lava flows southward for seventy miles as though following the twistings and windings of a river bed. This lava field is so extremely rugged and broken that a jack rabbit can hardly cross its borders except where man has built a highway.

At the terminus of the Malpais—as this lava stream is called—stretches the great expanse of burnt gypsum, known as the "White Sands," from its crystalline whiteness. It lies about halfway between Las Cruces and Alamogordo, and is at present a government park and tourist resort. It is eighteen miles long and three miles in width.

Many persons advance the theory that the same upheaval which destroyed the Grand Quivira resulted in the upbuilding of this glistening, sparkling expanse of sand that stretches along a low range of hills.

At the time of which I write, these sands were

notorious as the scene of numerous murders, in addition to the wiping out of the Nesbits. The sands are in perpetual motion, so that all signs of a murder and burial would be completely obliterated within a half-hour. Notable among these mysterious murders was that of Colonel A. J. Fountain, prosecuting attorney for that district. While enroute to Mesilla to attend court, he and his eight-year-old son disappeared at the White Sands, and despite careful search the only clue that was ever discovered regarding their disappearance was one of the shoes of the little boy.

The "Nickel-Plate Lady"

THE ROSWELL OF 1936 is, of course, very different from the town I knew in 1881. The site of the old horse corral is now occupied by an imposing courthouse, dignified in its classical architecture beyond what is usual in such buildings. The site of the old cow corral is covered with several buildings, among them being the armory of Battery A, New Mexico National Guard.

Married Life in Old Lincoln

SOME OF THE younger officers at Fort Stanton at that time were destined to rise high in military circles. General John J. Pershing was then a lieutenant stationed at the fort. He and his running mates, Lieutenants Paddock and Penn, were dubbed the "Three Green Peas," by August Cline, because of their being such persistent tenderfeet.

Others among the officers at the post in those days were Captain Thomas Cruse, Lieutenant Scott, Captain Rogers, Captain Bishop, Lieutenant Davis, Lieutenant Stetsenburg, Dr. Taylor, the post surgeon, and many others, who have since climbed to higher rank in either military or civil life.

While Lincoln, in 1883, was becoming more and more Americanized year by year, it was still largely a Mexican settlement. The number of "straight American" settlers would not have totaled twenty. In addition to John William and myself, I can now recall only the Dolans, the two Ellises, the Barbers, the Thorntons, the Cockrells, and the Boltons.

The American element showed quite a tally of unmarried men. The actual "bachelors" were Smith Lea, Colonel "Mickey" Cronin, Colonel George T. Bell, Governor-to-be George Curry, and several others whose names have escaped my memory.

A Cabin on the V's

MRS. LISNET WAS to meet General Pershing again. In 1913 he came back to Roswell, but not as a "green" lieutenant. He was on an inspection tour and stopped to inspect the New Mexico Military Institute which had been founded in 1890. He took occasion to revisit various places in the neighborhood which he had known as a young officer fresh from The Point and to look up those old acquaintances who survived.

When he learned that Mrs. Lisnet was still alive and in Roswell he expressed particular interest in seeing her. But the meeting occurred without pre-arrangement, on the street. When he saw her coming toward him he called:

"How do you do, Mrs. Lisnet! Remember me?"

"Sure, and that I do!" she answered instantly. "Ye're the leftinant that was always killing me pigs!"

Fortune Favors the Ex-Sheriff

E. A. CAHOON, John William Poe's associate in the organization of the *Bank of Roswell*, supplied the following information about the beginning of this pioneer institution:

The idea of a bank in Roswell was initiated by Will Prager, who made a trip to Albuquerque and interested S. M. Folsom (then president of the Albuquerque National Bank) in the idea of locating a bank in Roswell. Folsom made a trip down here in the fall of 1889, with one H. S. Beattie, and made his final arrangements with Jaffa, Prager, Poe, Lea, and Cosgrove for the erection of a building, and for the amount of stock the people in this section would take. The bank was to be opened early in 1890, but the building was not finished in time, and we did not start business until July 26, 1890. In the meantime, Beattie had deserted Mr. Folsom and been employed by the Reynolds banking outfit. So it eventually fell to me to come down to Roswell and start the thing off. We left Albuquerque the night of July 19, by train for San Antonio, N. M., a place now deserted, but which was about twelve miles south of Socorro. There we were to catch a branch line to Carthage, from which our mail used to get to Roswell. Our train, however, was late, and the Carthage train had left when we reached San Antonio, and we had to wire U. Ozane, who had the contract to bring us over, to come on down to San Antonio. That gave us a late start, and so that night we only got as far as Ozane's mountain ranch in the Oscuras. There were four of us in the party, in addition to Ozane and his driver, we having two four-horse rigs, and bringing the bank fixtures and furniture with us. The next day we crossed the Malpais, came by where Carrizozo now stands, and went on up the canyon to White Oaks, where we spent the night. The following day we went to Lincoln, leaving there very early in the morning, and the next day we got our breakfast at old man Cline's, at Picacho, and reached Roswell at five-twenty the afternoon of the 23rd.

The four of us in the party were S. M. Folsom, W. P. Metcalf, Fry (my clerk), and myself. We brought about thirty-six thousand dollars with us, six thousand dollars in silver, as there was no change in the country and we had been advised to bring quite a lot of it, as it would be hard to get afterward. This silver was carried in two two-inch boxes, under the front seat of the wagon in which I rode, and in a small grip strapped to me, I had thirty thousand dollars in currency and gold. As we were expected, I did not know what we might

run up against, and we were pretty well "heeled."
We were ready for any kind of trouble. However,
nothing happened. We arrived safely, found the
bank quarters yet unfinished, but placed our fixtures through Hill, the contractor, moved our safe
in (which had been sent over a month before by
freighters) and opened for business Saturday
morning, July 26, 1890. Our bank was located the
farthest from a railroad of any bank in the United
States at the time, with no telegraph, telephone, nor
express.

It could be truly called a frontier bank. It was
capitalized at fifty thousand dollars, and ten thousand dollars of the stock was subscribed for locally,
Jaffa and Prager taking twenty-five hundred dollars worth, and Poe, Lea, and Cosgrove a like
amount. Henry Milne took ten shares of stock;
Judge Stone, ten shares; Judge Richardson, five
shares; Frank Lisnet, five shares; and Roberts, who
was then running the Chisum ranch, was to take
ten shares, and be a director; but he "blew up"
about that time and left the country, never taking
his stock.

Our first board of directors was Mr. Poe,
Nathan Jaffa, Mr. Folsom, Judge Richardson, myself, Judge Stone, and when Roberts failed to
qualify, in September, we put in Mr. Hinkle.

You ask especially about our making the trip
over to Roswell. It was practically uneventful. I
remember that we all had to get out and walk up the
big hill, and that wherever we stayed at night, we
left the boxes of silver in the wagon. No one (ex-

cept ourselves) knew what we carried, and we did not inform anyone, although there was six thousand dollars that might have been carried away while we were sleeping.

In the forty-four years of the bank's existence there have been but five presidents—Folsom, Poe, Godair, Sr., Godair, Jr., and Cahoon.

At the time of John William Poe's burial, July 23, 1923, a brother Mason, Robert Kellahin, delivered the following appraisal of his friend's life and work:

Before concluding these ceremonies, and ere we leave this spot, now made sacred because it holds all that was mortal of our friend and brother, let us recall for a brief space his many virtues. Let us remember those qualities of mind and heart which have endeared him to every Mason, making each one feel that the sacred title of *Brother* had a deep and true significance when it was used by him.

Not that any weak tribute from our lips can possibly add to the lustre of that life which is now closed, or make the memory of that life more enduring in the hearts of those who are left behind. It was a life well spent in service, in work, in promoting the well-being and happiness of his fellow man; and nothing we can say can beautify or adorn the record that has been made. But for our own sakes it is worth while to review our associations with this man who has gone out from us and so, perhaps, more truly profit by an example of faithfulness of the performance of every duty. He dis-

played fearless courage in defending that which
he believed to be right, and exhibited an unflinching
integrity in all affairs of life which is seldom
equaled. He had all the characteristics of the really
strong man, and in his dealings with his fellows he
showed himself imbued with the kindness and sympathy that goes with strength.

We have never known him when he did not show
a due and proper reverence for sacred things, re-
specting with utmost care the rights and opinions
of others in matters spiritual. Yet, there is nothing
in his character that would make us remember him
as a sentimentalist. It would not seem fitting to
indulge, at this time, in sentimental reference to
our departed friend. Rather, would we voice, if we
could, the admiration, love, and esteem which his
brethren held for such a strong and virile character,
such a true and warm friend, and seek to realize in
some measure, what an inspiration his life has been
to those who were privileged to associate with him
during the many years he went in and out among us.

It might be said, with truth, that our community, with all its varied and increasing activities,
has been built around the life of John W. Poe; and
more than once, as the years have come and gone, it
has been remarked that Roswell was truly for-
tunate in having men of the type of John W. Poe
as its pioneers—men who were fearless, but just;
men who were instinctively moral and law-abiding
citizens; men who had the vision to build empires,
but yet laid their plans with care; forceful men,
who framed their purposes and never wavered

from them. Such a man was our late brother and many others who were associated with him in the early days of our history, and it is to them that we owe the measure of comfort and happiness we now enjoy.

We have our various civic organizations, it is true, but the foundation for that we now have was laid by those pioneer men who are passing from us one by one. As all the brethren well know, his Masonic affiliations were very dear to him, and his faithful and active service to Roswell Lodge Number 18 will ever be remembered.

He was one of the four who held that historic meeting in the fall of 1888 for the purpose of taking the initial steps to organize a Masonic Lodge in our comparatively new community. The other three have preceded him into the Great Beyond and now his going will complete the quartette on the Other Side.

To speak of the share that was taken by John W. Poe in the public affairs of the country would be to give, in detail, the history of this part of New Mexico. We cannot think of any movement of consequence in the upbuilding of Roswell and the surrounding country in which he did not take an active, and often a leading, part.

Brethren, we have today laid to rest one who spent himself in his work; one who, from the day he first trod the soil of New Mexico up to the very closing hours of his life among us, has been one of the chief bulwarks of our law and order; one of the stalwart leaders, upon whom we could depend at all times. Those who know the history of Roswell can remember well that there have been times when such men were sorely needed, and John Poe was one who never failed us.

He has been taken from us—why, we do not know. Where that strong and manly spirit is today we do not know, nor can we tell in what new sphere he may be prosecuting the endless search for Truth. But we do know that for many long years he has lived and worked among us, setting a standard of life which few of us, perhaps, can attain. We can see the lamps which he has lit along the pathway of life for us, and if we follow them with the same unswerving purpose, the same inflexible fidelity that he did they will, in due time, lead us to the end of a well-spent life, and we shall join him and those who have gone before in that glorious land that every good Mason looks forward to with hope and confidence.

Index